Career Planning
& Netw

10647262

Professional
Development Series

Author:

Aggie White, M.A.
Central Carolina Technical College
Sumter, South Carolina

SOUTH-WESTERN

✦ ™

THOMSON LEARNING

Australia • Canada • Mexico • Singapore • Spain • United Kingdom • United States

SOUTH-WESTERN

THOMSON LEARNING

Career Planning & Networking
By Aggie White

Executive Editor:
Karen Schmohe

Project Manager:
Dr. Inell Bolls

Editor:
Carol Spencer

Marketing Manager:
Chris McNamee

Marketing Coordinator:
Cira Brown

Production Manager:
Jane Congdon

Manufacturing Manager:
Carol Chase

Art and Design Coordinator:
Stacy Shirley

Cover and Internal Design:
Grannan Graphic Design, Ltd.

Compositor:
Electro-Publishing

Printer:
R.R. Donnelley/Crawfordsville

Gain the Insight to Professional Success

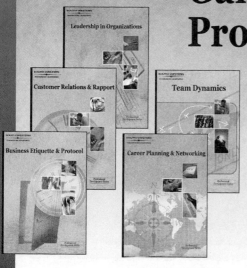

Keeping pace with today's competitive marketplace is a challenge.

Although technology has enabled us to communicate and produce in ways we never thought possible, there are other essential elements to achieving professional success. *The Professional Development Series* is a quick and practical resource for learning non-technical strategies and tactics.

0-538-72463-3	Business Etiquette & Protocol
0-538-72527-3	Customer Relations & Rapport
0-538-72484-6	Leadership in Organizations
0-538-72474-9	Career Planning & Networking
0-538-72485-4	Team Dynamics

The 10-Hour Series

This series enables you to become proficient in a variety of technical skills in only a short amount of time through ten quick and easy lessons.

0-538-69458-0	E-mail in 10 Hours
0-538-68928-5	Composing at the Computer
0-538-69849-7	Electronic Business Presentations

Quick Skills Series

Quickly sharpen the interpersonal skills you need for job success and professional development with the Quick Skills Series. This series features career-related scenarios for relevant and real application of skills.

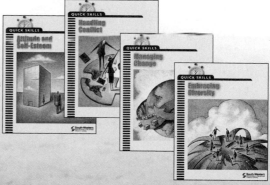

0-538-69026-7	Attitude and Self Esteem
0-538-69833-0	Handling Conflict
0-538-69839-X	Managing Change
0-538-69842-X	Embracing Diversity

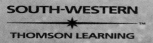

SOUTH-WESTERN
THOMSON LEARNING™

Join us on the Internet
www.swep.com

Contents

Preface

In the last decade of the twentieth century and the first decade of the twenty-first century, the American worker is facing stiff competition, an increase in the level of skills employers are seeking, and the demands of continual change in the workplace. The idea of one job for life is no longer an operable plan for today's worker. Once a person chooses a career, he or she must formulate plans to continually progress through that career. Chances are, however, that the individual will change careers a number of times during his or her lifetime.

Message to the User

Career Planning and Networking was written to assist anyone who wants to use a step-by-step process to progress through his or her career. The module is designed as a guide to provide an overview of the steps involved in the career planning process. The module also focuses on the importance of building and maintaining a strong, effective network that will support and assist a person throughout his or her career. This module also contains a Portfolio Project featured on page 69 that encompasses the key concepts presented in each topic. This portfolio can be used as a reference tool for career planning.

Features

Each topic begins with clear goals entitled "At the Core." A list of key concepts learned is presented at the end of each topic. A pre- and post-assessment activity is also included at the beginning and end of the module that may be used as a fun, nongraded activity. *Career Planning and Networking* is organized into six topics that cover an overview of the career planning and networking process, self-assessment and decision making, researching careers and networking, the job search, the job offer, and preparation for change. Online resources for further research are provided for every topic. Tips appear throughout the module to emphasize important concepts and present ideas for class discussion. A Portfolio Project is included at the end of this module that may be be used as a resource tool.

About the Author

Aggie White is an educator by profession. She graduated from The Ohio State University with a bachelor of science degree and taught in the field of education as an elementary school teacher; she also worked several years in business. Upon receiving a master's degree from the University of South Carolina, she moved to post-secondary education. She has served as an instructor and as department chair in the Office Systems Technology Department of Central Carolina Technical College for the last nine years. She currently serves as registrar for the college and continues to teach on a part-time basis.

Pre-Assesment Activity

Multiple Choice: Read each of the following statements carefully. Circle the letter of the best response for the following statements.

1. The standards or principles we use to help us make decisions or choices in our lives are
   a. societies.
   b. peers.
   c. value systems.
   d. missions.

2. A statement that describes what a company is, what it does, and how it envisions itself in relation to its market is a
   a. value system.
   b. mission.
   c. goal.
   d. market alignment.

3. When faced with making a decision and based on the importance of the factors involved in that decision, a good strategy is to
   a. verbalize.
   b. prioritize.
   c. personalize.
   d. quantify.

4. An excellent source of information about careers can be learned from
   a. college/career counselors.
   b. the Internet.
   c. government publications.
   d. all of the above.

5. The people who are connected to you through your career field
   a. are your career network.
   b. are a group.
   c. include only your friends and relatives.
   d. include only friends of friends and relatives of friends.

6. The person who is a teacher, coach, and helper, and who will help you learn about your career and career choices is a
   a. friend.
   b. mentor.
   c. relative.
   d. supervisor.

7. When planning a career, one should research
   a. vacation time.
   b. work relationships.
   c. job availability.
   d. all of the above.

8. A résumé should contain
   a. an objective.
   b. education/work experience.
   c. your name.
   d. all of the above.

9. A résumé that is organized in groups by types of experiences is a
   a. chronological résumé.
   b. curriculum vitae.
   c. functional résumé.
   d. none of the above.

10. An interview in which the interviewer(s) ask exactly the same questions in the same order to all the applicants is a(n)
    a. structured interview.
    b. unstructured interview.
    c. one-on-one interview.
    d. panel interview.

11. Appropriate attire for an interview includes clothing that is
    a. comfortable.
    b. conservative.
    c. clean.
    d. all of the above.

12. The purpose of the thank-you or follow-up letter is to
    a. tell the employer you are not interested in the position.
    b. ask for an interview.
    c. keep your name and qualifications fresh in the employer's mind.
    d. all of the above.

13. The atmosphere, or environment, in which the work of the organization is completed is the
    a. corporate culture.
    b. grapevine.
    c. communication system.
    d. organizational structure.

14. Upward communication is the pathway in the company communication system in which
    a. the supervisor communicates with the subordinate.
    b. the subordinate communicates with the supervisor.
    c. the peer communicates with the peer.
    d. all of the above.

15. Offerings by a company that have value for the employee are
    a. communications.
    b. values.
    c. competition.
    d. benefits.

16. A tax-deferred investment and savings plan for retirement that permits the employer to match what the employee invests is a(n)
    a. IRA
    b. 401(k)
    c. 403(b)
    d. Roth IRA

17. The economic term that describes the loss of something in order to gain something else is
    a. a gain/lose
    b. supply and demand
    c. negotiation
    d. an opportunity cost

18. When beginning a new job, a helpful strategy for a successful beginning is to
    a. use your senses to learn as much as quickly as possible.
    b. ask questions and analyze processes.
    c. read company manuals to familiarize yourself with the policies.
    d. all of the above.

True-False: Read each of the following statements carefully. Circle T if the answer is true, and F if the answer is false.

T F 1. A goal you are pursuing should be quantitative so you know if and when you have reached the goal.

T F 2. If there is a shortage of qualified workers in a career field, salary ranges will not differ.

T F 3. Newspapers provide very little information about companies and organizations, so you should avoid using them as a source.

T F 4. If a company is in litigation, the company's reputation, earning power, ability to hire and stability may be affected.

T F 5. Use a font size that is less than 10 for your résumé.

T F 6. When writing a solicited letter of application to a company or business, you do not know if a position is open.

T F 7. A letter of application should be one page and three paragraphs long.

T F 8. An interview is a meeting, usually face-to-face, between the employer and the job applicant.

T F 9. All interviews are one-on-one and face-to-face.

T F 10. The company grapevine is a rumor factory that is rarely accurate.

T F 11. Never use the word *negotiable* to answer the salary question on a job application form.

T F 12. The vertical movement from one level in a career field to the next is referred to as upward mobility.

1
The Career Planning and Networking Process

AT THE CORE
This topic examines:

➤ **DISTINCTION BETWEEN A CAREER AND A JOB**

➤ **ROLE OF PLANNING IN CAREER SELECTION**

➤ **IMPORTANCE OF CAREER PLANNING AND NETWORKS**

➤ **ELEMENTS OF AN EFFECTIVE PLAN**

➤ **DEVELOPMENT OF A PLAN**

areer planning and preparation can and will affect the quality of the jobs you choose and, more importantly, the satisfaction you will derive from your chosen career. According to the *Kiplinger Washington Letter*, December 1996, "People will have to take more responsibility for their careers . . . assessing their strengths and weaknesses, planning schooling, and job paths. The days are gone when just about anyone could step into a lifetime job with regular pay raises, promotions, and a good pension at retirement."[1] Therefore, planning becomes critically important as we enter the first decade of the new millennium.

A worker will spend approximately 2,000 hours a year for 40-plus years in the world of work, and that chosen path will have a dramatic effect on the quality of the worker's life. Therefore, you want to plan and prepare effectively for this journey through the world of work. Anticipate giving time and energy to planning your career by:

- Developing a comprehensive plan for acquiring the resources you will need for a specific career.
- Conducting a self-assessment of your values.
- Establishing your goals and committing yourself to a written plan with timelines.
- Researching careers and professions.

- Preparing for the job search process.
- Evaluating job offers.
- Anticipating how you will adjust to the many changes in the workplace
- Planning for promotions and advancements.
- Planning for job and technology changes.

Each step of career planning is important. This module examines the five-step process to planning. Each step is significant in the total picture of where you want to go in your career. Each step will affect your decision making and will affect your quality of life during your working years. The better prepared you are to meet the challenges presented in each of these areas, the better able you will be to make effective decisions. Preparation comes before success—even in the dictionary!

Courtesy of ©PhotoDisc

Equally important to the careful planning of your career is the development and cultivation of a network of people who will provide advice, insight, direction, support, and motivation as you progress through the stages of your professional life. Therefore, in addition to examining career planning, this module also focuses on the importance of networking to your career plan.

Career or Job

An important distinction to be made regarding career planning is the difference between a job and a career. A job is a position for which you are employed. You are assigned responsibilities, provided guidelines as to expectations, and paid a specified amount of money. A job may last days, weeks, months, years, or a lifetime. A career, however, is the pursuit of a profession or a specific line of work. Within a career, you may have many different jobs. A career implies growth in knowledge about your profession or line of work and a progression with the assumption of more responsibility in each job you hold. A career also implies dedication to self-imposed standards of professionalism and pride in your work performance. Therefore, a career requires growth, progression, and standards of professionalism. In order to meet these challenges, career planning becomes a commitment you must make.

The Role of Planning

We do not plan for the past. We do not plan for the present. We plan for the future.

As Charles Kettering, the industrialist, said, "I expect to spend the rest of my life in the future, so I want to be reasonably sure what kind of future it is going to be. That is my reason for planning."[2]

Planning is a critical element in all aspects of life. However, it is especially critical in the development of your career. To plan is a future-oriented concept. You should have already planned for today. When broken down into its simple steps, planning sounds easy; but few people do it. They just allow things to happen, with no direction or guidance to help them arrive at a destination.

Why planning is important in career development? In the routine things you do everyday, you unconsciously plan. When you drive to work or school, you unconsciously plan your route. You get to your destination because you are following a route you know well.

However, a career is not a routine or minor occurrence in life. It is a journey that requires planning to reach the goals or destinations you set for yourself. How do you get from where you are to your career destination? If you did not plan your trip, how would you ever arrive at where you want to go? But before you plan your trip, you must know your destination. If you do not set a destination, an objective, or a goal, how do know when you have arrived? Likewise, if you do not set a destination or goal for your work life, how can you evaluate the success of that life? Evaluation is a very important element of all decision making.

Courtesy of ©PhotoDisc

This does not mean that the destination you set when you are twenty is cast in concrete and will never change. Of course, you can change the direction you are taking and the path you have chosen. At some point, events will occur, circumstances will change, and environments will evolve to cause you to change your focus and/or destination. Therefore, career goals must be flexible enough and realistic enough to adapt to change.

Career planning will have an impact on the quality of your career. Planning will determine the level of satisfaction you experience; it will determine how well you handle change and whether you are prepared for the promotion and advancement opportunities that come along in the world of work.

Job satisfaction is a crucial aspect of maintaining a positive attitude about your career. Planning allows you the opportunity to make wise career choices, which will affect the quality of your career and contribute positively to your job satisfaction. Every job has its frustrations; your goal is to be employed in a work environment where you derive more satisfaction than frustration. You will realize this only by planning your career.

The Career Planning Process

The career planning process is an in-depth, detailed, and thought-provoking process that will require your time and energy. It is a sequential process and is best accomplished by following the established progression through each step. This *Career Planning and Networking* module will examine in-depth the five-step process in career planning. Following is a brief overview of each step.

1. Self-Assessment to Decision Making: Career planning begins with self-assessment. Remember that a destination, a goal, or an outcome is critical to any plan. Before you can set a goal or an outcome, you must decide what you want to do. Assess your values and abilities, and determine what opportunities, resources, and avenues are available to you to accomplish your goals. Identify what is important to you or what you value, and use this information to guide you in making effective decisions.

2. Career Research and Networking: Career planning requires that you learn about the different career options available to you. Researching careers can be fun and can broaden your knowledge of what is available in the world of work. Nearly unlimited resources for exploring careers and career options are available today. By researching careers, you are better prepared to determine what you want to do and what you do not want to do.

A network is equally important to your career. A network is a system of interconnectivity where one element supports, assists, promotes, or redirects other parts of the system; all parts of the system are often interdependent. There are many different types of networks in our world today—for example, computer networks, television networks, and cable networks. A career network refers to a group of people connected to you through your career.

Career networks are important because you do not live in a vacuum. In addition, you cannot possibly know everything that is happening in the world around you. You must rely on people from different arenas to help keep you informed about what is happening in areas with which you are not familiar.

When beginning to develop a network, you want to turn to the people around you such as family, friends, and acquaintances. Each individual's network will be different simply because families, friends, and acquaintances are different. As your network expands, you begin to include other people you meet and with whom you interact. You may include instructors with whom you connect. You may include coworkers, employers, and subordinates with whom you have worked or with whom you are currently working. As you become involved in professional organizations, colleagues and contemporaries may become essential members of your network. You may include those you have met through sports, recreation, or entertainment. Each person you meet has the potential of becoming a part of your network.

Building and maintaining a network may be the single most important aspect of effective career planning. The members of your network are critical as you begin to expand your knowledge base and grow professionally.

Courtesy of ©PhotoDisc

3. The Job Search: The job search is another important aspect of career planning and is actually a two-step process itself. The first part of the process for the search involves preparing yourself physically and emotionally and creating certain documents that will communicate to prospective employers your qualifications for the job. Also, you must learn about the company at which you are applying for employment. The basic documents required for the job search are the résumé, the letter of application, and the reference sheet. Learning about the company involves finding out what goods it produces or what services it provides. Your network becomes an important resource now, providing you with important information as you prepare to enter the often competitive world of the job search.

In the second step of the job search process, you must prepare for the interview and its follow-up procedures. Preparing for the interview means that you practice answering interview questions and identify the appropriate clothing to wear. Another aspect of this step of the career planning process involves the follow-up procedures, such as sending a thank-you letter and contacting the company to learn its decision concerning the position for which you applied.

4. The Job Offer: When offered a job, you must evaluate the offer to see if it fits into your plan. Does the offer match the values and goals you have set for yourself? You also must consider the company benefits, salary, opportunities for promotion, location, and corporate culture. Not all job offers are positive. When you view your employment as a career and not just a job, the evaluation process becomes easier. Factors such as location, salary, benefits, and workplace environment are closely related to your job satisfaction. You make quality career choices when you are prepared to appropriately evaluate the offers that are made to you.

One of your goals should be to avoid getting into a position where you have to take a job just because it is offered to you. This type of situation usually does not lead to meeting your career objectives. You may need to take a short-term job to help you or your family through a difficult time. However, avoid accepting a long-term job just for the paycheck.

5. Planning for Change and Career Advancement: Change is a given in the world today. Change in the workplace is inevitable and rapid, and it affects everyone. Because change is so much a part of today's work world, you must be prepared for any changes that occur in your professional life. The better prepared you are with the skills an employer wants and needs, the more options you will have in dealing with the changes that come. Mergers, reorganizations, downsizings, and layoffs may affect your career. Therefore, you must develop strategies to help you meet the challenges change will bring to your career.

Plan for developing effective task management skills. You must be an effective and efficient employee to accomplish your objectives each day. You must take time for personal and professional growth so you are continuously learning over the span of your career. This is known as life-long learning.

Finally, a very important aspect of career planning as it relates to changes in the workplace involves the ability to understand and handle success and failure. Failure happens to everyone and is an important aspect of a person's career if viewed as an opportunity. Enjoy the success and learn from the failures.

The ability to handle the many changes that come along in a career is also determined by the extent of the initial planning. You should have a plan for your personal and professional growth so you are prepared for change. For example, the more education you have, the better prepared you are for whatever reorganizations or layoffs may come your way. You must also be able to adjust to changes that are beyond your control. The more flexible you are and the more options you have, the better able you are to handle these changes. Change often presents an opportunity for growth. Being prepared means taking advantage of negative situations and enhancing your chances for professional growth.

In your career planning, include goals for progression in your career field. This involves gaining experience, knowledge, and responsibility. Prepare and position yourself to take advantage of any opportunities for career promotions. Identify and develop the resources, skills, and abilities you need for promotions and advancements that arise.

Anticipate the costs involved in being prepared for job opportunities, such as time away from your family and tuition for education. Many companies today recognize the value of employees who want to improve their skills. Often companies will support and encourage employees by assisting them

Courtesy of ©PhotoDisc

financially or giving them time off from work to pursue educational goals or to take advantage of professional development activities. This support and encouragement is a benefit that should be considered when evaluating a job offer.

A critical aspect of career planning is to recognize when the time and situation is right to make a job change. Relocation, job advancement, better working conditions, and more challenging responsibilities are all good reasons to make a change in employment. Know when and how to make a change. You must be able to recognize the signs that tell you it is time to move to another position. You also must know how to leave a job in a professional way. You want to look just as good leaving a job as you did arriving.

Fundamentals of an Effective Plan

You should approach planning in a systematic, yet flexible way. Several characteristics of effective planning should be incorporated into your career planning. These will be critical in your developing a workable, understandable, and realistic plan.

- **Take the appropriate time to plan.** Planning is not an overnight process. It may take days, weeks, months, or years. It is not a one-time event, but a continuous process.
- **Commit your plan to paper.** By putting your plan in black and white, you are forced to verbalize and visualize what you want to accomplish. Being able to say and see your goal increases your buy in and, therefore, your commitment to the goal. Your chances of succeeding increase with the degree of commitment you have to the goal.
- **Be sure your plan is comprehensive.** You may choose to put your plan in an outline form, but it must be complete. Include the necessary resources—time, energy, money you will need to commit to accomplish your goal or reach your destination.
- **Identify timelines for accomplishing tasks.** By defining a time frame for accomplishing tasks along the way, you are setting deadlines for yourself. Deadlines can provide motivation. Deadlines also give you an opportunity to pat yourself on the back for completing a step in the journey toward your goal.
- **Arrange your plan in a logical sequence.** A logical sequence prevents you from having to do a task a second time because another task

should have been completed first or from getting midway through one task before you realize that an essential element is missing.

Courtesy of ©PhotoDisc

- **Identify any obstacles to your plan.** All facets of life contain barriers and speed bumps. Identifying them may be difficult, but you do not need to identify them all. Just be aware that they exist or identify them as they arise.
- **Identify possible solutions to overcome these obstacles.** Knowing ahead of time what the barriers are allows you the time and energy to plan for them and to determine how you will avoid them, eliminate them, or turn them to your advantage.
- **Identify resources for helping you accomplish your plan.** Resources come in many different packages. Anything or anybody that can assist you in accomplishing your plan is considered a resource.
- **Evaluate your plan.** Set the criteria that will determine the success of your plan. Assess whether you have met the standards you have set.
- **Include flexibility in your plan for the inevitability of change.** You now understand that change will occur. The original Fortune 500 was published 50 years ago. Today only a few of the original companies are still on the list, and those that are still counted are in different businesses.[3] Being aware of what is occurring in the workplace and the changes that are affecting your chosen career is critical in your career plan. You do not want to be the worker who committed himself to the manufacturing of the buggy whip when the industry was moving toward the automobile.

Development of the Plan
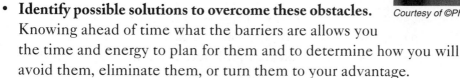

As you progress through the topics in this module, you will begin to develop a plan for your career. You must commit yourself to the process, which means you will need to schedule time to assess your strengths, skills, abilities, and talents; to question yourself about what is important to you; to determine in what direction you want your interests and talents to take you; and to create a statement to guide you as you begin your career search. Once you have determined your destination, you will look at ways to research and gain information about your career choice. You will prepare yourself and the documents required for the job search. You will learn to evaluate a job offer against the standards you have set to determine whether it meets your requirements. Finally, you will learn that as your career progresses, you must be prepared for change, plan for your progression, and know how and when to change jobs to best meet your career objective.

RECAP OF KEY CONCEPTS

- A career is the pursuit of a profession or a line of work and may involve many jobs and job changes. A job, however, is a position for which you are employed. A job may be short-term or long-term, but a career is a lifetime pursuit.
- Planning is determining a destination or goal and then creating a process by which the goal can be reached.
- The career planning process is important because it provides the structure and direction a person needs to stay focused on his/her career goal. A network offers support and provides advice, insight, direction, and motivation.
- The elements of developing an effective career plan are taking the time to plan, committing the plan to paper, making the plan comprehensive, identifying timelines, arranging the plan in a logical sequence, identifying obstacles and solutions, identifying resources, establishing methods of evaluation, and ensuring the plan has flexibility.
- The development of the plan will evolve as you progress through the sequential five-step career planning process.

2
Self-Assessment and Decision Making

AT THE CORE
This topic examines:

➤ **THE IMPORTANCE OF SELF-ASSESSMENT**

➤ **THE DEFINITION OF VALUES AND VALUE SYSTEMS**

➤ **THE DEFINITION OF A MISSION STATEMENT**

➤ **THE DEFINITION OF A GOAL**

➤ **ELEMENTS OF AN EFFECTIVE GOAL**

➤ **FUNDAMENTALS OF EFFECTIVE DECISION MAKING**

When you decide to take a trip, you begin to assess your resources to be sure you have all the requirements for the trip. Suppose you decide to take a vacation to Australia. You should do some research to be sure you have the necessary papers, enough money, the appropriate tickets, and whatever clothing and personal items you might need to take on the trip. If you did not acquire a passport, you would not be permitted to leave the United States; and if you did not acquire a visa from the Australian government, you would not be permitted to enter Australia. You would want to assess your financial resources to see if the trip would even be feasible. Would you want to spend your vacation worrying about whether or not you could afford it? You would also want to consider appropriate clothing for the trip. Suppose you decided to visit Australia in June, and you planned to take shorts, T-shirts, and your favorite pair of sandals. You might be a miserable traveler because June is in the middle of the Australian winter. Research and assessment is the key to effective planning.

Although planning for a trip is important, planning for your career is even more important. Just as you must assess your resources to see that you have everything you need for a successful trip, you must assess your resources to see that you are prepared for a successful journey toward your career destination.

Courtesy of ©PhotoDisc

This topic investigates the process of self-assessment in the setting of meaningful goals, which will help you get to where you want to go. This topic also discusses the importance of your values in creating a mission statement, which will set the outline and plan for your life. From your mission statement, you will set goals; the goals you set will affect the decisions you make. Once you have determined your goals, you will need to develop strong time and task management skills to help you along your journey.

Self-Assessment

As you begin looking at yourself and your resources, you may want to take some simple assessment inventories to gather insight into your personality. These assessments will help you determine the types of work for which you are best suited. You possess a set of characteristics that make you unique and, at the same time, make you similar to others in what you like to do. Many assessment instruments can assist you in finding a career that suits your interests and/or personality. However, they may not determine your ability to perform well in that particular career. You may possess personality traits and interests that a nuclear scientist possesses, but that does not necessarily mean you have the intellectual ability or the desire to become a nuclear scientist yourself. Most of the assessment instruments provide categories, or types, into which the participants fall. From the types/components/categories, you can determine what kinds of work situations you might enjoy. Two popular inventories are the Myers-Briggs Type Indicator® and the Strong Interest Inventory®.

The Myers-Briggs Type Indicator is one of the most popular tests on the market. You can use it to gain a quick understanding of personality variables to consider as you research your career options.[1] The results provide you with an inventory of preferences in how you tend to center your attention to the outer world of people or things or to your own inner world, how you acquire information, how you make decisions, and how you deal with or orient yourself to the outer world. Trained career counselors must give this inventory. Most college counselors and career service providers are able to administer the assessment. If they cannot, they should be able to direct you to someone who can.

The Strong Interest Inventory is a classic career inventory. This test assesses your interests (the best predictor of career satisfaction) and compares you to six broad fields of employment.[4]

Numerous personality tests are available over the Internet. They are fun but usually only confirm what you already know about yourself. Online Resources, page 68, lists several web sites to visit for quick personality inventories.

Values and Your Value System

Self-assessment must include a determination of your values. You know that what you value is of some worth or is important to you. Whether you are aware of it or not, however, you develop a set of values—those things that are important to you. Some people may decide that education is important to them. Others may decide that money, health, prestige, or fame is important. Whatever you decide is important to you becomes the basis for your set of values—or your value system.

A value system, therefore, is composed of the standards or principles that you use to make decisions or choices. A value system develops over a lifetime and is influenced by many factors. Naturally your parents and family have a great influence on helping you develop what you believe to be important. They also help you set the standards by which you are guided. Society impacts your value system. The friends you choose, the television shows you watch, the religious organizations to which you belong, the books you read, the heroes and heroines you admire all have an impact on your value systems. Many external factors, events, people, and experiences will influence what you consider to be important (the standards or principles that guide you) and, as a result, the decisions you make.

A Mission Statement

Once you have determined what your values are, it is time to write a mission statement. Many companies today have written a mission statement that describes what the company is and does and how it envisions itself in relation to its market. The mission statement is based on what the company values or thinks is important to the success of the company. In many cases, a company will state how it plans to accomplish its tasks. Cisco, one of the wealthiest companies in the world, has the following mission: "Shape the future of the Internet by creating unprecedented value and opportunities for our customers, employees, investors, and ecosystem partners."[5] Notice that the mission statement includes what the company plans to do and how it plans to accomplish its mission. Cisco plans to "shape the future of the Internet"; then the company states how it plans to do that. The word *by* is key. This mission statement is the reason for the company's existence.

You should develop a mission statement that explains who you are and why you exist and what you will do to be the person you want to be. The mission statement should be founded on your value system. Remember to add how you will accomplish your mission. Use the word *by*. When you have completed your mission statement, write it on a 3x5 card. Carry it with you, and refer to it often.

Once you are consciously aware of your value system and have written your mission statement for life, you are ready to set the goals that will get you to your destination. Only when you know what you want to do with your life and why you want to do it, can you create effective, purpose-driven goals.

Setting Goals

A goal is a target at which you aim, a result for which you work, an objective you want to reach. The more a goal is supported by what you value, the more committed you will be and the harder you will work to reach it. When you know your destination and you have the resources to make the trip, you can begin to set the goals to help you get there. When you plan, you always set a goal, though you may not even be aware of it. As you decide to accomplish something, that something becomes your goal.

TIP Goals are critical. If you don't know where you are going, how will you know when you get there?

You should set your goals with a solid knowledge of your values and mission. If your goal is in conflict with your value system and your mission statement, you may not have the motivation or desire necessary to reach that goal.

Keep the following guidelines in mind as you set your goals.

- **Personal:** Goals should be personal. Set a goal because *you* want it. Never set a goal because someone else wants you to do it. If you set a goal to be a doctor, set the goal because *you* want to be a doctor, not because your mother, father, or significant other wants it. Your motivation and desire to be a doctor cannot come from an outside source; it must come from within you.

- **Quantitative:** You must be able to determine if you have met a goal—a "Yes, I did" or "No, I didn't." Therefore, something must be included in the goal that can be quantitatively measured. For example, if you set a goal to save money, how will you know when you have reached the goal? "To save money" is a goal that will never be met because you did not specify a measurable amount. However, "to save $5,000" is a goal that can be measured; it includes a success criterion.

- **Realistic:** The goal must be possible to attain. You want to be an astronaut who will travel to the moon next year. That goal may be realistic for an astronaut currently in the NASA program, provided a moon mission is scheduled for next year. The goal is unrealistic for a college freshman with no experience. Setting a realistic goal is important because success in meeting the goal is the objective. Goals should be challenging, but they still must be within the realm of possibility.

- **Specific:** State your goals in specific terms so you can visualize the actual accomplishment of the goal. For example, your goal is to be successful. But be successful at what? Describe what you will be doing. "I will own my own trucking firm with 55 trucks delivering goods throughout the southeastern part of the United States. The company will be making $1.5 million a year by December 2005." A specific goal tells what, when, where, and how much. On December 31, 2005, the goal is either met or not met.

Courtesy of ©PhotoDisc

- **Limited In Time:** In other words, put a date and time on the goal. If you do not put a time limit on the goal, you have no motivation to accomplish it. Again, make the time limit realistic, but specific. "I will buy a new car (state the color, model, make, and so on) by May 1, 2004." On May 1, 2004, you have either met the goal or you haven't.
- **Value-Based:** Always return to your value system to set your goals. If you set a goal that is in conflict with what you believe to be right and important, you will either struggle with the guilt of pursuing the wrong goal for the wrong reason or you will lose interest because the goal is not important to you.

Goals can and should be set in all areas of your life. Personal, professional, educational, financial, and even social goals can be set. A career goal is one to which you are willing to commit time, energy, and resources (both financial and personal).

Resources For Goal Setting. Once you have set a goal, you must evaluate what is required from you to reach your goal. You must also assess the resources you have available to help you reach your goal. If you find you do not have the resources necessary to reach your goal, you must determine how you will gather the needed resources.

For example, you have set your goal to become the director of an Information Systems department of a 500-employee-plus corporation by June 2008. You are currently an information systems programmer in a mid-sized organization and have an associate degree in computer technology. As you evaluate your needs, you find that directors of IS departments usually have at least a master's degree in computer science and have been systems analysts and many times assistant directors before becoming IS directors. Therefore, you know you must obtain a bachelor's degree and a master's degree, which will take a minimum of three years if you attend college full-time.

Look at your resources. Does your current employer offer tuition assistance to employees who are interested in furthering their careers? Are student loans an option? Research the financial resources available to help you reach your goal. Does your local college or university provide the courses and program you will need? Could you take advantage of Internet-based courses to get the degrees required? Now you have a sub goal. Again, make it specific and time-limited. "I will receive my master's degree in computer science from York University by June

2005. Your primary goal is still your career goal—to obtain a position as a director of Information Systems by June 2008. However, now you have created and developed a secondary goal—an educational goal—to support and help you attain the primary goal.

Courtesy of ©PhotoDisc

When you have created the goal, check to be sure it meets the six criteria of a goal. Is it *personal?* Yes, you are doing it for *you*. Is it *quantitative?* Yes, you either get a master's degree or not? Is it *realistic?* Yes, you have given yourself four years to earn the master's degree and another four years to find the position. Is it *specific?* Yes, you have named the type of organization, the position title, the university, the program of study, and the time limit. Is it *limited by time?* Yes. Is it *value-based?* Yes, a career is valuable and important to you, and the director of Information Systems in a 500-employee-plus corporation is an important career progression for you.

An important element of setting goals is that the goal must be flexible. In other words, do not set such a rigid goal that it cannot be altered to meet the changing needs of both you and the workplace. Eight years is a long time in the world of technology. Much can happen and change. Director of Information Systems may be an out-dated position in eight years. Computer science may change. Your interests may change. Allow flexibility in redefining your goal.

Elements Of Effective Decision Making

Every step you have accomplished in this module—understanding the importance of self-assessment, your value system, and your mission statement and setting effective goals   are all leading you to the process of making effective decisions that will support and assist you in the planning for your career.

Decision-making is simply making choices. The important factor in good decision-making is analyzing the options and then deciding which option provides the best solution to the situation. Notice the word *best*. The reality is that most decisions involve some sort of risk—the risk being that the decision will be a bad one. Remember that not all decisions you make will be good ones.

One of the advantages of setting goals is that you have already removed many of the obstacles to effective decision-making. The research you do prior to setting the goal, when you examine available resources, eliminates the "What ifs. . ." and the "Yes, buts. . ." If your goal is to purchase a car next year and your goal meets all six of the criteria, your research would have determined the following: 1) what you can afford; 2) how you will pay for the car; 3) how much money you can get for your present car by selling it direct or trading it in; 4) what repairs you must make before selling the car; and 5) what you will pay for insurance, taxes, and so on. The decision of which car to buy is not a difficult decision to make because you have set a plan in motion. You are not purchasing based on emotions or impulse.

Your value system is at the core of how you make decisions or choices. It is present when you choose between right and wrong. It is present when you choose between studying for a final exam and going to the movies with friends. It is present when you choose whether to spend money on clothes or a software program or to save the money for next semester's tuition. When you choose between two or more options, your value system kicks in and assists you in making the choice. Consciously or unconsciously you list the advantages and disadvantages of each option, weigh the consequences, and make your choice.

To be certain you make the best choice, write down your comparisons. For example, you need reliable transportation to get to school and your job every day. You have conducted research, finding two cars. One is a four-year-old used red sporty convertible; the other is a new dark blue sedan. Here is your list.

Convertible	Sedan
Advantages	**Advantages**
The color	New—low mileage
Used car	Lower insurance rates
Fun to drive	Uses regular gas
$200 per month car payment	4-door
Lower property taxes	Full warranty

Convertible	Sedan

Disadvantages
Higher insurance rates

Uses high-octane gas

2-door

70,000 miles

Disadvantages
$250 per month car payment

Higher property taxes

Lower resale value

What are the factors that would help you choose which car to buy? Is it only the amount of money the car will cost you? In the cost, did you include insurance, property taxes if you are required to pay them, maintenance, and cost of gasoline? Did you think of the practicality of each car? Or did you perhaps think about the fun and prestige of driving a sporty, red car? Your value system will help you make the decision. But if you end up feeling guilty about the choice you made, you are in conflict with your value system.

Strategies for Effective Decision Making

Write down your options. When making a decision, use the following technique that Ben Franklin, inventor and statesman, used. At the top of a piece of paper, write the action you plan to take. Fold the paper in half. On one half, write all the reasons for taking the action you have described. On the other half, write all the reasons for not taking the action. Whichever side has the most reasons should be your choice of action.[6] Sometimes, however, this strategy may be a bit simplistic.

Gather as many facts about the decision as you can. The more information you possess, the better decision you can make. Write down a list of factors that will influence your decision. Try prioritizing that list. What is the single most important factor in the decision? What is second, third, and so on? For example, you are planning to buy a house. What are the ten most important factors to you in your search? Suppose you list the following: three bedrooms, two baths, affordable cost, two-car garage, bonus room, eat-in family kitchen, family room, swimming pool, large lot, and hardwood floors. What is the number one feature on which you are not willing to compromise? Perhaps it is the cost. Perhaps it is the number of bathrooms or bedrooms. Make a list of the options you want. Prioritize them from the most important to the least important. Those items that occur at the bottom of the list are the features on which you are willing to compromise. Those at the top of the list are critical features for you without which you would not be satisfied with the outcome of the decision.

In decision making, try to be objective. Keep the emotion or impulse out of the choice. Although a gut instinct or a hunch can be valuable, cold, hard facts are much more reliable for making effective decisions.

RECAP OF KEY CONCEPTS

- ◆ Before choosing a career, it is important to take some assessment inventories. These inventories will help you determine if your abilities, interests, and personality are compatible with the demands of your chosen career. Two popular assessment instruments are the Myers-Briggs Type Indicator and the Strong Interest Inventory.
- ◆ A value is something of worth or something important to you. Value systems are the standards or principles you use to make decisions or choices in life.
- ◆ A personal mission statement describes who you are in terms of what type of person you want to be and how you plan to become that person. A company's mission statement describes what the company is and does and how it envisions itself in relation to its market.
- ◆ A goal is a target at which you aim, a result for which you work, an objective you want to reach.
- ◆ An effective goal should be personal, quantitative, realistic, specific, limited in time, and value-based.
- ◆ The fundamentals of effective decision making are analyzing the options available and determining which option provides the best solution.

3
Researching Careers and Networking

AT THE CORE
This topic examines:

➤ **SOURCES OF CAREER INFORMATION**

➤ **INDIVIDUALS TO INCLUDE IN A NETWORK**

➤ **TOPICS FOR RESEARCH**

➤ **THE USE OF THE INTERNET TO RESEARCH A CAREER**

➤ **SOURCES OF INFORMATION ABOUT COMPANIES AND ORGANIZATIONS**

➤ **"NEED-TO-KNOW" INFORMATION ABOUT A COMPANY**

 ow that you have written your mission statement and determined your values, it is time to establish areas of interest and determine possible career choices from those interests. This will require some research on your part. You will need to investigate what careers match your values and interests. As you research various aspects of the careers, you will utilize as many sources of information as possible so you have sufficient knowledge to make an effective decision. In addition, you will explore what information to gather about careers and organizations that employ workers in your chosen field.

Sources Of Career Information

You can use many sources to learn about careers and career opportunities. Some sources are better for learning about local or regional prospects and provide more specific information. Some sources are most effective in a national or global sense. Use as many sources as you can to learn as much as possible.

College Career Counselors. A college career counselor's specialty is knowledge about careers and what the skills, abilities, interests, and so on, a person must have to be successful in a career. The career counselor can also direct you to interest tests to help you determine what you might like to do. These career interest inventories contain questions about what you enjoy doing, how you enjoy working, and where you enjoy being. The results match your interests with the interests of people who have chosen particular careers. This does not mean you have the skills and abilities to perform the tasks necessary to become a successful worker in that career, but the results give you some career options where the job requirements match what you enjoy doing. The career counselor is an excellent resource with whom to start your career search.

Government Publications. The Department of Labor publishes many annual volumes and manuals that can assist you in your career research. One of the publications is the *Dictionary of Occupational Titles*. This is a listing of all the job titles found in the United States. The Department of Labor also publishes a *Guide for Occupational Exploration*, which places jobs in categories, or classifications. Under the classifications, the jobs are categorized into occupations that require similar skills, talents, or characteristics. These are useful sources for discovering a type of job that matches your interests and abilities.

The Internet. Once you have a category of types of careers that interest you, go to the Internet. Select a search engine or a search directory. Narrow the focus of your search so you do not become over-loaded with hundreds of choices and become frustrated in your search. You may have to use several different key words to find the information you need. The Internet provides the opportunity to explore what seems to be an unlimited wealth of information about an unlimited richness of topics with just the click of a mouse. You can explore this vast library of knowledge by using a web browser such as Internet Explorer or Netscape. Within the browser, you can use search engines such as AltaVista or Yahoo, which are web sites that create and maintain a database directory of other web sites. These sites allow you to search the database for information on your particular topic. The more specific you are about your topic when querying the search engine or database, the more likely you will be to narrow your search and retrieve the information you need. At times, the search may become frustrating; a search engine may provide you with thousands of sites that address the topic you are researching. You would not be able to physically look at each of these sites. So the more limited you can make your request and the more specific you can be about your topic, the better chance you have of finding the site that provides the information you need.

Courtesy of ©PhotoDisc

TIP When working with search engines on the Internet, be patient. Try to avoid getting frustrated in your search.

Your Career Network

Probably the single most important resource you have about careers is your network. As discussed in Topic 1, a career network is composed of those people connected to you through your career field. You are surrounded everyday by people who can be of great benefit to you in your career search. Parents, friends, parents of friends, classmates, instructors, relatives, relatives of friends, friends of relatives (literally anyone with whom you come in contact) are possible sources of information about your career.

A network is very much like a garden. Before you plant, the garden bed should be rich in nutrients and the soil prepared for the plants to grow. In the same way, you must be prepared to nurture your networking relationships by:

- **Checking your attitude.** Is your outlook positive? Are you open to new ideas? Are you willing to put in the time and effort necessary to foster the relationships?
- **Developing human relations skills.** Are you a good listener? Are you sensitive to others? Can people trust you to do what you say you will do? Do you look forward to meeting new people? Are you a resource for other people? Do you accept assistance graciously? Do you care about others?
- **Being committed to self-improvement.** Do you look for ways to better yourself? Are you committed to life-long learning? Do you have a plan for self-improvement? Do you know how you need to grow?

Like a garden, a strong career network includes symbiotic relationships that have deep, healthy roots that survive in a nutritious, rich environment. This will not occur without nurturing the relationships. Subsequent topics will be discussing how to create and establish a strong, healthy network.

Courtesy of ©PhotoDisc

Importance of a Network. A strong and effective network provides you with support, guidance, direction, and advice at certain times in your career. A good network is available when you begin to look for a job, when you decide to make a career change, when you are experiencing change by external forces, when you need advice to handle a difficult problem, or when you feel the need for motivational or moral support. A strong network is a critical element to begin to develop as you work on your career plan.

Once you have an idea of what you want to do, ask the members of your network if they know of anyone currently working in that career field. A person in your network is sure to know someone. Obtain that person's phone number or e-mail address. Contact him or her. Ask for an appointment to discuss that person's career. Prepare your questions well so you can learn as much as possible from this contact person. You will glean invaluable information.

You want to cultivate a variety of people for your network. Each person is important and can be a valuable resource as your career progresses.

A mentor is a teacher, coach, or helper who will teach you about your job and career. Mentors are those experienced in a career field who take young or inexperienced people under their wings; mentors share their knowledge and provide guidance and advice. A relationship with a mentor may last a lifetime. Usually, mentors are well-respected in their field, due to their position, job knowledge, and willingness to share and advise. Qualities that identify a good mentor are strong job skills with experience and knowledge of the job, the ability to teach and share effectively, and the willingness to share their expertise with you. The last attribute is perhaps the most important. In order to determine if a person will make a good mentor, you must be very observant and listen carefully. Look for individuals who take pride in the quality of their work ,who are good listeners, and who can clearly articulate answers to your questions.

The person who knows everyone and is known by everyone is the person who has a stack of business cards of important contacts in his or her field. This person may be active in the local Chamber of Commerce or in nonprofit organizations or may serve on various boards of directors. The "one who knows everyone" is important because he or she can connect you to the right person or to someone who can direct you to the right person to solve your problem or answer your question. This person in your network does not have to be a personal friend, but you should know who this person is and understand how valuable he or she can be to you.

Becoming a member of a professional organization may be the single most important decision you make in your career. A professional organization is a group of people who join together to promote their chosen profession by developing a mission statement and setting goals and standards by which members operate. Every profession has a professional organization, and most have national, regional, and state chapters of that organization. Doctors, lawyers, CPAs, teachers/educators, engineers, administrative assistants, and architects—all have professional organizations. By being an active member, you receive up-dated information about your profession and have an opportunity to attend state, regional, and national conferences, which usually provide opportunities to learn about changes and innovations in your field. You have the opportunity to meet other members who are working in your profession. What an opportunity to learn and grow and develop that important network—and expand it to a state, regional, and even national level.

An advocate is someone who supports you and speaks up for you—promotes you and your interests. An advocate becomes an important member of your network when you cannot promote yourself or your ideas, perhaps when a promotion or job elimination is being considered. A strong advocate sees that your interests are protected when you are not available or not consulted about the change.

A professional friend has all the typical characteristics of a friend and is a colleague in your profession or career area. In other words, this individual is loyal and trustworthy; this person keeps your confidence and is there for you when times are tough. This friend is also truly happy for you and supportive when times are good. Usually, this is a two-way street—you fill this need in your friend's network and he or she fills yours. This person is important because you need a sounding board, a support person, a place to go when you hit a speed bump in your career. Remember that this relationship is based on trust; you must develop trust over a period of time, and it must be nurtured and protected.

Your network is very important to the development, growth, and strength of your career. A network does not develop overnight, and it requires constant vigilance to keep it active and strong. These issues will be discussed in later topics.

Topics to Research for a Career

You have established some places to go to get information. Be prepared to check several sources. You may find conflicting information or be unable to gather all the information you need from one source. Now that you know what sources are available, what information will be of most value to you?

Job Availability. This is a critical factor in career planning. Nothing could be more discouraging, disappointing, or frustrating than putting time and money (your most important assets) into education or preparation for a career only to learn that a scarcity of jobs exists in that field. For example, suppose you decide you would like to become a paralegal and work for an attorney. Your research of the job market tells you that the attorneys in your town are not hiring paralegals but are looking instead for competent legal administrative assistants. You then have to make a career decision. If you choose to stay where you are currently living, the paralegal field is not a strong option for you. Your better choice would be to earn a degree as an administrative assistant. However, if relocation is not a problem and the attorneys in that location hire paralegal assistants, then you should pursue your education in that field.

Courtesy of ©PhotoDisc

Job Titles. Many positions may have similar responsibilities but a variety of job titles. As you research job titles, be sure you have included all the titles used in your field of interest. There are thousands and thousands of job titles—different titles for the same job and different job duties and responsibilities for the same title. For example, a secretary, an administrative specialist, and an administrative assistant may all have the same job duties and responsibilities. However an administrative assistant may have added responsibilities depending on the type of office in which he or she works.

Potential for Advancement. You also want to learn what the potential is for progressing in the career path you have chosen. Most employees begin at an entry-level position. With time, experience, and education, a career path leads you through several levels to many jobs. Hopefully, each level requires more expertise and responsibility so you grow in breadth and depth of knowledge about your job; assume more of a leadership role in your career; and earn the respect of your supervisors, peers, and subordinates. For example, as a rookie police officer, you may be walking a beat or riding in a patrol car. Your next step may be as a sergeant who supervises others and plans work schedules. Your next step may be as a lieutenant. Each move requires you to know more about your career. Your responsibilities grow, offering new challenges, as you advance in your career.

Salary Range. You certainly want to investigate and determine a salary range for your job field. Money is important to everyone. People work to earn a living and to provide a good life for their families and themselves. Therefore, you should know a reasonable amount to expect from an employer. However, be aware that wide ranges of salaries exist within careers and jobs. The region of the country, an urban or rural environment, the education, the background and experience, and the availability of qualified employees in a field all affect salary ranges. For example, a teacher in the states of New York and California earn more money than a teacher in Mississippi or Arkansas. However, before making a judgment about that statement, realize that the cost of living is also different in those states. In addition, if there is a shortage of qualified workers in a career field, you may discover a salary range higher than what you expected.

Education Requirements. Research the level of education required in your career field. A high school diploma may not provide you with the skills needed for the technically challenging jobs and careers available. Therefore, research the education requirements of your career interests. Do you need certificates or diplomas in the field? Does the job require an associate degree? a bachelor's degree? a master's degree? a doctorate? Or perhaps you do not need formal education, but the education provided by experience in the field.

Sources of Information on Companies and Organizations

As you plan your career, you need to learn about the companies, firms, and organizations that will use your talents and skills. Careers are not always self-contained. In many cases, you will be hired to work within a firm. For example, all graduates from law school do not open their own firms or join another law firm. Many lawyers have successful careers in businesses, in the government, and in many sectors of the workplace. Therefore, you want to research where your career choice could possibly take you.

The sources of information about companies and organizations are nearly limitless. Your ability to learn as much as you can about a company may only be limited by your imagination. Some sources are obvious; some are not.

The Internet. With the increased emphasis on e-commerce today, most companies have a web site that provides extensive information about the company. For example, you may learn about a company's product(s), history, mission statement, CEO, and board of directors; you may also find a listing of employees, e-mail addresses, and job openings with job descriptions. Some companies and government agencies even provide an on-line job application form that you can complete and e-mail to the company. This source of information will only become greater as the Internet and e-commerce grow.

Newspapers and Magazines. The business sections of newspapers provide extensive information about local companies, especially information that might not be found on the Internet or from other sources. The business section also covers successful people in the business world. Who has been promoted, or who has received a prestigious award? Magazines such as *Business Week* and *Forbes* are good sources of information about national and global companies.

A Company Prospectus. By writing or calling a company, you can request a prospectus. This report provides useful information by telling you how the company is currently performing. Remember, however, that the company will probably emphasize the positive aspects and glide over the negative.

Courtesy of ©PhotoDisc

The Chamber of Commerce or Better Business Bureau.

Your local Chamber or Better Business Bureau (BBB) can be an important source of information about local companies. The Chamber can provide you with extensive information about a company, and the BBB can tell you if the company uses ethical and fair business practices. Customers contact the Better Business Bureau when they are dissatisfied with the services provided by a company.

Your Network. By asking your family, friends, mentors, and professional colleagues, you can learn anything you want to know about a company—its reputation, current employees, products, CEO, corporate culture, job openings, and contact persons. Someone you know knows someone who knows about the company. Find out who that person is, and contact him or her. Learn all you can.

"Need-to-Know" Information

Once you have established your career path, you begin to search for a job. You also research the companies for which you might like to work. But for what type of information are you looking? What do you need to know to make a wise decision?

- **Stability of the Company:** Stability does not necessarily mean how long a company has been in business. Stability means the reliability or dependability of the company. Is the company sound and secure?
- **Earnings Trend:** Is the company a successful and profitable company? Does it provide a quality product, whatever that product is? Will the company be in operation tomorrow?
- **Litigation:** Are any lawsuits pending? These may affect the reputation, earning power, hiring trend, and stability of the company.
- **Merger or Take-Over Rumors:** Have you heard any rumors or facts or hints of a merger or take-over? If so proceed with caution. Usually in a merger, the lesser of the two companies loses employees. If only one position is available after a merger, the person employed by the stronger of the companies is most likely to retain the position. Therefore, if the lesser of the two companies is your employer, you may be out of a job. Also the last person hired may be the first to be let go when a merger or downsizing occurs.

Courtesy of ©PhotoDisc

- **The Turnover Rate:** This may be difficult to determine, but try. A high turnover rate usually indicates employee dissatisfaction with a company. Many reasons may explain this dissatisfaction. An investigation of a low turnover rate usually shows that the employees are long term, happy with their jobs, and loyal to the company; a low turnover rate indicates a stable and productive company. Not surprising, a company may be very willing to share with you the fact that it has a low turnover rate; however, it may be reluctant to admit it has a high one.

The more you know about your chosen career and the possibilities of jobs, career growth, and career satisfaction, the better prepared you are when you begin actively looking for a job. As you move along your career path, you encounter many branches. Although you start working toward one goal, other doors of opportunity may open, resulting in a different path leading in a different direction. This does not mean you have failed to reach your goal; it only means that your goal has changed. That's okay!

RECAP OF KEY CONCEPTS

- ◆ Many sources are available for information about careers (for example, college career counselors, government publications, and the Internet).
- ◆ Your career network is composed of those people connected to you through your career field—parents, friends, parents of friends, classmates, instructors, relatives, relatives of friends, and friends of relatives.
- ◆ When researching career paths, investigate job availability, job titles, potential for advancement, salary range, and level of education required.
- ◆ Sources of information about companies and organizations include the Internet, newspapers and magazines, company prospectuses, your local Chamber of Commerce, the Better Business Bureau, and your personal network of family and friends.
- ◆ Information you want to know about a company includes the stability of the company, the earnings trend, pending lawsuits, rumors of mergers, and the turnover rate.

4
The Job Search

AT THE CORE
This topics examines:

➤ **PARTS OF THE RÉSUMÉ**

➤ **THREE TYPES OF RÉSUMÉS**

➤ **THE LETTERS OF APPLICATION**

➤ **THE JOB APPLICATION FORM**

➤ **THE INTERVIEW**

➤ **TYPES OF INTERVIEWS**

➤ **PREPARING FOR THE INTERVIEW**

➤ **ENDING THE INTERVIEW**

➤ **THE THANK YOU LETTER**

➤ **EVALUATING THE INTERVIEW**

 orkers today make seven to eight career changes in their lifetime. Therefore, the process of seeking a job is not a once-in-a-lifetime experience. You will probably do it over again. Job seeking is a process that includes several steps. Each one can be critical in helping you find the best possible job within the personal and professional parameters you have set.

You need to develop a résumé that catches the interest of a potential employer, and create an effective letter of application that will accompany your résumé. In some cases, you need to complete the job application form. Once you are granted an interview, you want to make a favorable first impression. Send a thank you letter after the interview to keep your name and skills at the forefront of the employer's mind. These are all critical steps in your job search.

The Résumé

A résumé is a document that contains information about a job applicant's previous employment experience, educational background, related skills, and abilities. The purpose of a résumé is to get an interview. You usually present your résumé to a potential employer, also including a letter of application, which is sometimes referred to as a cover letter. The most common method of getting the résumé into the hands of a prospective employer is by first-class mail; however, as times and technology change, other methods are now used. E-mailing and faxing your résumé is acceptable if requested to do so by the employer. You may also post your résumé to your personal web site. If you choose to publish your résumé this way and direct potential employers to your web site, be sure your web site is professional and represents you as you would like your employer to know you.

Employers spend approximately 30 seconds looking at a résumé. Therefore, your goal in creating a résumé should be ease of reading. Be sure important points are easy to find, and emphasize items you want the employer to focus on.

Parts of the Résumé

A résumé may be divided into seven parts: heading, objective, work experience, educational experience, special certification or software skills, awards/recognitions, and references.

- **The Heading:** The heading of the résumé should contain your name, address, home telephone number, and e-mail address, if appropriate.

TIP If you have an answering machine, be sure the message the caller hears is professional and appropriate. If including an e-mail address on your résumé, be sure the address is professional and appropriate as well.

- **Objective:** This section of the résumé is optional. It is not essential to the effectiveness of a résumé, but it helps focus the employer's attention to the goal you have set.

- **Work Experience:** This section details information about your work experience. You want to provide the length of time you were employed, the name of the organization for which you worked, and the city and state in which the company is located. Provide your job title. Under the job title, list the duties you performed while on the job. Begin each description with an action verb. This method of presentation makes it easy for the employer to skim the résumé to find the job skills you have acquired.
- **Educational Experience:** In this section of the résumé, include all the schools and colleges you attended, when you attended, and what degrees you earned. You may want to include some of the courses you took if they relate to the job you are seeking.

> **TIP** If you include information about the high school from which you graduated, do not include the date of your high school graduation. With this information, an employer may make a decision about you based on age before he or she has even met you. A person's age can be determined by a high school graduation date. This does not apply to college graduation, however, because college students are all different ages.

If you did not receive a high school diploma but earned a GED, state when and where you were awarded the GED.
- **Special Certifications or Software Skills:** In the world of work today, employers are seeking employees with specific skills and/or knowledge. In this section of the résumé, list any software and the versions with which you have a working knowledge.
- **Awards/Recognitions:** If you have received any special awards or recognition from school, work, or community activities, you should list them. Many employers are looking for employees with a variety of interests who are involved in the community.
- **References:** The reference section is usually last on the résumé. You should state that your references are available upon request. You can present a potential employer with your list of references at the interview.

Courtesy of ©PhotoDisc

References fall under three categories: professional and/or work-related, educational, and personal.

Types of Résumés

There are three basics types of résumés: the chronological, the functional, and the curriculum vitae. Each type is used to arrange educational and work experience in a different manner to best emphasize the skills of the job seeker.

- **Chronological Résumé.** The chronological résumé is arranged with work and educational experiences in reverse chronological order; that is, the most recent work or school listed first, followed by the next most recent, and so on. Job seekers who have limited experience or experience that directly relates to the job they are currently seeking find this a very effective résumé format.
- **Functional Résumé.** The functional résumé is organized into types of experiences. This résumé is best used by job seekers who have held numerous positions and have a variety of experience.
- **Curriculum Vitae.** The curriculum vitae is more extensive than the functional or chronological résumé. A curriculum vitae includes not only educational and work experience, but also publications, speeches, presentations, awards, and recognitions. Educators primarily use this type of résumé.

Selecting an Effective Format. When selecting a format for your résumé, remember two factors: 1) Most résumés are skimmed rather than read thoroughly by the employer. Thirty seconds is the average amount of time an employer spends looking at a résumé. 2) The employer must be able to find your strengths and qualifications quickly. Therefore, place this information strategically, and emphasize the qualifications the employer is seeking.

Style and Presentation. Your résumé represents you to a potential employer. The reader cannot see you; therefore, he or she forms an impression of you and makes an instant decision about you from the messages your résumé sends. This impression is made in approximately seven seconds. Never give an employer the opportunity to form a negative impression. Therefore, your résumé must be perfect. Not only does the content and the grammar you use create an impression, but the paper, the font (size, style, and color) and the placement of the information on the page also influences the reader's impression of you. This impression determines whether you get an interview.

Paper and Ink. Select a good quality bond or parchment paper. Keep the look professional by using neutral colors of white, gray, or beige/cream. When purchasing bond paper, keep in mind the more cotton or linen fiber in the paper, the higher the quality. Use black ink. The envelopes should be the same color, weight, and quality as the paper used for your résumé.

Font Size and Style. When selecting font size, do not use a font less than 10 points or greater than 14 points. You never want to make the reader have to work hard at your reading your résumé. Choose a style of font that is easy to read. Remember, you do not want the reader to struggle; he or she may not take the time, quickly eliminating your résumé from consideration.

TIP After printing your documents, be sure to let them dry thoroughly before folding them. If the ink is not dry, it will leave an impression, or mirror, of the printed document on the page.

The Letter of Application

The document that usually accompanies the résumé is the letter of application or cover letter. Use the letter of application to "sell yourself." Provide the reader with information that is not on the résumé, emphasize important skills and abilities from the résumé, inform the reader/employer about how you learned of the position, and ask for an interview. Do not use the letter of application to repeat what is in your résumé. Your aim is to make the reader want to meet you by scheduling an interview. The letter of application also provides the opportunity to demonstrate your written communication skills. The interview will give you the chance to demonstrate your oral communication skills during the interview.

Types of Letters of Application. There are two types of letters of application. A letter written to a company that is actively looking for potential employees is called a solicited letter of application. You may have learned about the position through an advertisement in the newspaper, through a friend, or through an intracompany memo about job postings. You know the position is open. Companies often solicit résumés and letters of application in newspaper ads but use a post office box or a drawer number or letter as an address. This type of ad is called a blind ad. As an applicant, you do not know and cannot research the name of the person to whom you address the letter. The appropriate salutation in this case is *Ladies and Gentlemen.*

With the second type of letter of application, you do not know if a position is available. You are inquiring to find out. This is called an unsolicited letter of application. The company is not actively seeking applicants for a position. Your objective in sending an unsolicited letter is to place your name and qualifications before the company. There may be an opening presently, or one may become available in the near future.

Style and Presentation. The letter of application should be one page and about three paragraphs. In the first paragraph of a solicited letter of application, describe how you learned of the position. In the first paragraph of the unsolicited letter, provide the reader with a short description of the position for which you are seeking. Ask if such a position is available.

The second paragraph of both solicited and unsolicited letters of application may include any of the following information:
- Whatever skills you have that you know are required to perform the job
- Any skills you know the employer needs but are not listed on your résumé
- Why you believe you are the best candidate for the position

In the last paragraph, conclude the letter by asking for what you want, which is the interview. Provide information to make it easy for the employer to contact you.

The letter should be printed on the same weight, color, and quality of paper you used for your résumé.

The Job Application Form

The employer will supply you with a job application form. You may pick it up from the company, or the personnel department may mail it to you. You may also find it on the company's web site, download it, key in the information, and return the completed form to the company via standard mail or e-mail.

The job application form should be accurate and complete. Do not leave any sections blank. Use the letters *NA* (not applicable) if the requested information does not apply to you.

The Interview

An interview is a meeting, usually face-to-face, between an employer and a job applicant. It is a question-and-answer session, the purpose of which is to establish that the qualifications of the applicant meet the needs of the employer. The interview also allows the applicant to determine if the position and the company matches his or her needs.

The interview is one of the critical factors in determining whether you receive a job offer. Interviews can take various formats. Preparation is the secret to a successful interview. Practicing the answers to typical questions helps you build confidence and lessen the nervousness that accompanies an interview. Your appearance and the first impression you make with the interviewer is very important. Consider the interview as an opportunity to learn as much as you can about the job and the company. The interview is a two-way street. Be sure information is flowing in both directions.

When the interview is over, evaluate the effectiveness of your performance so you can improve any areas of weakness. Assess your performance. Ask yourself questions similar to the following: What questions did I answer well? What was the most difficult question I was asked? How would I answer that question if I were asked it again? Also take the opportunity to keep your name and qualifications in front of your interviewers by writing a thank you letter within 24 hours of the interview.

Types of Interviews

There are basically two types of interviews—structured and unstructured. During a structured interview, the interviewer asks exactly the same questions in the same order to all of the applicants. Structured interviews allow all the applicants to have the same opportunity to present their qualifications; structured interviews also eliminate any possibility of favoritism or discrimination. The unstructured interview, however, is more informal, and questions may be asked randomly. The interviewer may choose a question based on the answer an applicant gave to the previous question.

TIP Do not become too relaxed during an unstructured interview.

Format of the Interview. Most interviews are face-to-face. They may be one-on-one; that is, one interviewer and one applicant. It is not uncommon today to have a panel interview; that is, one applicant to a panel of interviewers (three to six interviewers). Questions are usually prearranged, and each interviewer may ask several questions. A head interviewer usually facilitates the interview.

When distance is a consideration and travel is prohibitive, employers may conduct an interview over the telephone in a conference call. Voice and oral communication skills are critical in this situation. Advancements in technology are offering new options for long-distance interviews. Telecommunications equipment is being used in some instances with audio/video transmission. This does require expensive equipment on both ends of the interview, but the interviewer and applicant can see and hear each other in real time. Using the Internet and the software package NetMeeting, the interviewer and the applicant each place in inexpensive camera on his or her personal computer; both parties can then see and hear each other in real time.

Improvements in technology will greatly impact the format of the interview. The methods mentioned here today may not be commonplace; however, in the future, you may find face-to-face interviews a thing of the past.

Preparing for the Interview

Research. Preparing for the interview begins with researching the company with which you are applying. Use your network, the Internet, the Chamber of Commerce, newspapers, business magazines, and the company prospectus (if you have time to acquire one). Know the company's product. Try to learn the names of top management and their positions. Try to discover your interviewer's name and position. Investigate the history of the company. Who are the company's competitors? Read the company's mission statement. Learn as much as you can.

Appearance and Attire. An interviewer makes a decision about you in 7 to 12 seconds. Plan ahead. What will you wear? Choose your attire with care. Be sure it is professional, comfortable, clean and conservative. Everything should fit properly.

Women: Choose a navy, gray, burgundy, black, or taupe suit or dress with a jacket. Choose the color and style that is most flattering for you. Hose should either match the color of your suit or be beige or taupe. Shoes should be black, navy, taupe, or burgundy with a heel no higher than 2 inches. Select accessories carefully. If you choose to carry a purse or portfolio, be sure it matches your other accessories.

Men: Select a suit in navy blue or charcoal gray with a white, long-sleeved shirt. Your tie should be a conservative print on a dark red or navy blue background. Socks should be black and rest high enough on the calf that bare skin does not show if the leg is crossed over the knee. Select accessories carefully.

> **TIP** While at the interview or researching the company, the applicant should carefully observe what appears to be acceptable to the company. Hair, teeth, breath, body, and clothes must be impeccably clean. Make a trial run to the location of the interview. Plan to arrive ten minutes early at the interview location.

Preparing for Interview Questions. The best way to prepare for interview questions is to practice. Develop a list of possible questions. Your local library or bookstore has many books that contain common questions. The Internet is a great source of interview questions. Next, develop appropriate answers. Practice the answers. Practice the answers while you are driving to school or to work. Practice in front of a mirror. Have a friend or family member ask you the questions while you practice the answers.

Generally, interview questions cover several areas: ice breakers, personal interests, educational preparation, and work-related experience. Two types of questions may be asked: closed and open questions. Closed questions require one- or two-word answers.

Open questions require a candidate to explain, express an opinion, or describe a situation. In other words, the applicant must organize his or her thoughts and develop sentences and paragraphs in order to effectively answer a question.

The Civil Rights Act of 1973 and subsequent addendums to the law have made questions about some areas illegal for the interviewer to ask. It is illegal to ask any questions about race, gender, age, ethnic background, or religious beliefs. Not all interviewers are aware of the illegality of some questions. If you are asked an illegal question during an interview, you have several options. 1) You can answer the question. 2) You can ask how the answer to the question relates to the job duties and responsibilities. 3) You can state that the question is illegal and you decline to answer. Options 2 and 3 will probably eliminate you from consideration for the position. If the company asks illegal questions deliberately or out of ignorance of the law, you may not want to work in that environment.

Ending the Interview

Be alert for an indication from the interviewer that the interview is over. A hint that the interviewer is finished asking questions is when he or she asks if you have any questions. The interviewer may state how and when the decision about the position will be made. In order to prevent any confusion, ask the interviewer what the next step will be. Ask if you may call in a week or two if you have not heard regarding a decision. Find out how you will be notified. Having all this information prevents your wondering whether or not to call to inquire if a decision has been made.

When the interview is concluded, stand, thank the interviewer for his or her time and for considering you for the position, shake the interviewer's hand, and leave. Thank anyone else who assisted you when you arrived.

The Thank-You Letter

Within 24 hours of the interview, write a thank-you letter to the interviewer. If more than one interviewer was present, you may send a letter to each, or you may send one letter to the lead interviewer and mention the others in the body of the letter.

In the first paragraph of the letter, thank the interviewer for his or her time and for considering you for the position. In the second paragraph, you have several options. You can stress something you wanted to emphasize but did not have the opportunity to do during the interview. For example, perhaps you were not pleased with the way you answered a question. Take this opportunity to answer it again and answer it well. Or you might want to list again the skills and abilities you have that make you "perfect" for the job. In the third paragraph, restate the understanding you had with the interviewer about what happens next.

The thank-you letter is also an opportunity to let the interviewer know if you are not interested in the position. Explain you reasons. An interviewer will appreciate knowing this as soon as possible so he or she does not waste time considering you, only to have you turn down the job offer later.

Be sure to sign the letter. The letter should be written on the same weight, color, size, and quality of paper you used for your résumé and letter of application.

Evaluating the Interview

With any new experience, you must evaluate what you have accomplished in order to grow and improve your performance. This is true of the interview process. It is essential that you review your performance so you can improve for your next interview.

Develop a written list of questions to ask yourself after the interview. Answer them immediately after the interview. By writing out your answers, you accomplish two things: 1) You have a record of who did or said what. 2) You have a review sheet if you should be asked to return for another interview.

RECAP OF KEY CONCEPTS

- The parts of the résumé are the heading, the objective, work experience, educational experience, special certifications or software knowledge, awards and recognition, and references.
- There are three types of résumés. The chronological résumé is arranged with work and educational experiences in reverse chronological order. The functional résumé is organized into types of experiences. The curriculum vitae is more extensive in listing work and educational experiences and is used primarily by educators.

- Your résumé represents you to a potential employer. Select good quality bond or parchment paper. Use black ink. Use a 10- to 14-point font.
- There are two types of letters of application: solicited and unsolicited. A solicited letter of application is written when you know a company is actively looking for applicants to fill a position. An unsolicited letter is written to a company when you do not know if a position is available, but you want to get your name and qualifacations before the company.
- Your letter of application should be on the same color, weight, and style of paper as your résumé. It should be one page and about three paragraphs in length.
- A job application form provided to you from the employer should be accurate and complete.
- The interview is a meeting, usually face-to-face, between an employer and a job applicant. It is a question-and-answer session to determine if the qualifications of the applicant meet the needs of the employer and vice versa.
- When planning what to wear to an interview, your primary consideration should be that your clothing is professional, comfortable, clean, and conservative.
- An effective thank you letter should include an expression of appreciation for the interviewer's time and consideration, emphasize why you are the perfect candidate for the position or re-answer a poorly answered question, and a restatement of what happens next if you want the position.

5
The Job Offer

- ➤ **THE CONCEPT OF CORPORATE CULTURE**
- ➤ **HOW TO DETERMINE THE CORPORATE CULTURE OF A COMPANY**
- ➤ **BENEFITS PACKAGES OFFERED BY COMPANIES**
- ➤ **FACTORS IN RESEARCHING SALARY AND WAGE**
- ➤ **THE MEANING OF OPPORTUNITY COSTS**
- ➤ **THANKING YOUR REFERENCES**

When you have received a job offer from a company, you must evaluate what the company is offering you. That offer means more than just the amount of your salary or hourly wage.

Every corporation has a corporate culture, whether the company is made up of 2 people or 200,000 people. This culture determines the atmosphere, or environment, in which the work of the organization is completed. A company's culture is rarely written down, and it may take a long time to develop. It is important that you fit in to the culture of the organization for which you work.

Many companies offer benefits of some kind to employees. These benefits can range from paid vacations to extensive retirement plans and health plans. Obviously, benefits have value. You must determine what value these benefits add to the job offer over and above the amount of pay you receive. You should consider the pay, the corporate culture, and the benefits when making a decision about whether to accept a job offer.

Once you decide to accept the job offer made by a company, you should thank your references for their part in helping you obtain the job.

Corporate Culture

Culture is defined as "the ideas, customs, skills, arts, etc., of a given people in a given environment."[7] Therefore, a corporate culture is the accumulation of unwritten rules of behavior, values, rules of engagement/procedures, and so on, that influence the way business is conducted in the workplace. All organizations develop a corporate culture, no matter how small or how large the company. For example, in Company A, new ideas may be encouraged, creativity rewarded, initiative valued, and the out-of-the-box thinker promoted. Company B, however, prefers business being done the way it was in the past. Employees' new ideas are not encouraged, initiative is considered rebellious behavior, and out-of-the-box thinking is not considered necessary to the success of the company.

Some organizations may emphasize customer service as their most important asset; this idea then drives all decisions made within the company. At the other extreme, an organization may believe that the bottom line, or profit, is the only factor that is important. All business decisions are made based on how these decisions impact the profitability of the company. Some companies may believe that competition and rivalry among individuals are the best methods of operation; others may emphasize and depend on teamwork as the key to accomplishing the goals of the company.

Determining a company's corporate culture before accepting a position with the company is to your benefit. If you are a highly creative person and reward for innovative ideas is a motivator for you, you probably would not want to accept a position with Company B in the previous example; you could be very unhappy. Be sure the environment in which you choose to spend your professional life agrees with your values and your life's mission.

TIP You want to fit in with your company's culture—8 hours a day, 40 hours a week, and 2,000 hours a year is a very long time to be unhappy, dissatisfied, and/or frustrated.

Those things you value in life should match (or at least not conflict with) the values of the company for which you choose to work. For example, you have accepted a position with Company Z. You soon learn that the company places an extraordinary value on the bottom line. In order to save the high cost of cleaning up the toxic waste products it generates, the company is illegally dumping them. You believe in the importance of clean air, water, and soil and consider this dumping an unethical practice (let alone illegal). Your values are in conflict with the values of the corporation and the corporate culture. You had better start looking for a new job.

Courtesy of ©PhotoDisc

The communication system within a company can often tell you about the corporate culture. Information travels in three directions in a company. Information travels upward from the subordinate to the supervisor, downward from the supervisor to the subordinate, and horizontal from peer to peer on each level. When communication is not open in these three directions, the company grapevine takes over and becomes very active. This rumor mill is generated due to poor or clogged communication channels.

When a subordinate feels comfortable discussing problems openly with his or her supervisor, sharing good and bad news, the upward communication channel is open. When a supervisor shares decisions made by upper management, accepts input and implements suggestions from the workers, listens carefully to what the workers say (and do not say), and respects the workers, the downward communication channel is operating well. When a peer feels comfortable discussing problems, procedures, and methods of how to work together more effectively as teammates, the horizontal channel of communication is open.

When all three channels function effectively, there is no reason for the grapevine to carry the information. All information is shared at all levels and in all directions. Therefore, a healthy corporate culture has an open communication system, where sharing is valued and respected.

How to Determine the Corporate Culture

How do you find out what the culture of a company is? This is not an easy task. The interviewer is rarely going to share with you the negatives of a company. In addition, the interviews are usually standardized, so you have little opportunity to learn about the corporate culture then. However, most good interviewers will ask if you have any questions. This is your opportunity!

- Determine, if you can, the turnover rate. Dissatisfaction with the corporate culture is one of the main reasons people leave a company.
- Determine the reward system if you can. How are people evaluated? How are employees motivated? What aspects of performance are emphasized? How are people promoted? What are the criteria used for promotion?
- Determine what the supervisor really wants. If the supervisor is present at the interview, ask questions about his or her expectations of your performance. How will you be evaluated?

Another way to determine corporate culture is to use your network. Someone knows someone who works for the company in which you are interested. It may be a friend of a relative, a college friend, or a relative of a friend. Find someone who has been with the company more than a year. Talk with as many people as you can at all levels of the organization.

Remember, your purpose is to learn as much as you can about the unwritten values, behavioral expectations, reward system, and so on, of the company. From what you learn, you can analyze and evaluate whether you think you fit in with the corporate culture. Decide if a company's culture matches your values, thereby valuing your work? This is one of the many factors that goes into your evaluation of a company's offer.

Company Benefits

A benefit is an offering by a company that has value for the employee or aids the employee is some way. The offering is over and above the salary or wage the employee is paid for performing a job.

Many American organizations realize that hiring qualified and capable workers means providing attractive benefits. Researching the benefits provided and having an idea of their value of is critical in evaluating and finally making your decision about a job offer. A company that offers no benefits may be at a disadvantage in being able to attract quality employees. If a company does not offer benefits, it may need to make a substantial salary offer to compensate for the lack of benefits. On the other hand, a company that offers a comprehensive benefits package may be able to offer a quality employee less in salary because the company is offering more in benefits.

Vacation/Leave. Although paid vacation, sick leave with pay, and paid personal leave are common in many businesses, they are still considered a benefit. Many companies require a probationary period of employment before benefits are available. Some benefits increase or accrue the longer an employee stays with a company. For example, after the first year of employment, an employee may accrue a week's paid vacation. After two years, the accrual may be two weeks. Employees who have been with the company 15 or 20 years may receive as much as four to six weeks paid vacation per year.

The same is true of sick leave or paid personal sick days. You may earn so many days per month or year. If you do not use all the days you accrue, you may be able to accumulate them to a maximum number. For example, suppose you are given 1.5 days per month in sick leave. At the end of the year, you have accumulated 18 days. Suppose you only used three days. You have 15 days that carry over to the next year. The company may, however, establish a policy that limits the numbers of days you can accrue, such as "up to 180 days of sick leave." It would take you ten years to accrue the 180 days, provided you did not miss any days of work due to illness during that ten years. Many companies pay you for unused sick days when you retire. This could be a substantial amount of money if you have worked for a company for many years.

Bonuses. Many companies reward their employees for exceptional work or for cost-effective ideas. A company that performs exceptionally well over the fiscal year may give out bonuses to employees. Bonuses are usually provided as a reward or to motivate employees to continue their exceptional performance. Bonuses may be based on a percent of salary, wage, or commission; or they may be a flat rate.

Courtesy of ©PhotoDisc

Educational/Professional Development. Companies who want employees to improve their skills and abilities may provide funding for educational courses, seminars, and workshops. Many times an employer will either pay for the course or reimburse the employee upon successful completion of the course. In some cases, an employer may even give a raise to the employees who successfully meet the standards or outcomes the employer has set. The employer may place a stipulation on the funding of the educational or professional development opportunity by requiring employees to stay for a designated period of time after completion of the course work.

Health-Care Insurance. Health-care insurance is the number one benefit most desired by employees; however, it can be extremely expensive, especially to employers with fewer than 50 workers. Employees usually prefer to choose their own doctor and to have a fixed amount to pay for prescriptions. There are a variety of health-care options. Two are discussed here.

Courtesy of ©PhotoDisc

Under the Health Maintenance Organization (HMO) plan, the patient chooses a participating primary care physician. The physician provides routine and pre-ventative care. The physician also coordinates the total health care of the patient. Usually, the patient pays a small percentage of the bill or a fixed rate of $5 to $10 per doctor's visit. The patient is not required to complete any forms.

Under the Point-of-Service plan, the patient is provided a list of doctors who participate in the plan. Patients may choose a physician on the list and then pay a percentage of the visit, usually 15 to 20 percent. Benefits may be restricted and some tests and treatments may not be covered at all. The patient must pay up front for all services provided by the physician. The patient must also complete a form in order to be reimbursed for the remaining 80 to 85 percent of the doctor's fees.

Although health-care insurance may be costly to a company, it can be a valuable benefit to the employee. It is a benefit worth considering when it becomes part of the job offer package. Purchasing health-care insurance as an individual can be very expensive; you may find that you have to spend up to $600 per month. That means $7,200 per year out of your pocket. When you add that amount to the amount of money an employer is offering, the job offer may become more appealing.

Life Insurance. When people enter the workplace and begin to earn a living and provide an income for their families and themselves, they assume some responsibility for protecting their family's future in case of their death. Even if you are not the primary breadwinner of your family, your income still provides a quality of life you would want to maintain if your family lost your income. Many companies today offer life insurance as a benefit. It may be a year's salary, a percentage of your salary, or a specific dollar amount. As your income changes over the years, you should evaluate the amount of life insurance you carry so your family, who is dependent on your income, is adequately compensated for the loss of your income should anything happen to you. Many types of life insurance, such as term and whole life are available. You should select the type that best fits your needs.

Retirement/Pension Plans. Social Security is a federal benefit established in the late 1930s to assist people as they retire, and to help disabled workers and widows and orphans of workers. Many people today wonder whether a social security fund will be available when the baby boomers retire. The issue of privatizing social security to allow participants to invest their own funds or a portion of their funds is part of this discussion. Whatever the outcome of these issues, social security alone will not be sufficient to maintain the quality of life you establish during your working years. You must begin to plan and save for your retirement years. It is never too late or too early to begin a personal retirement fund.

Your company may also have a pension or retirement plan to assist you. Federal and state agencies have retirement plans, which usually require a stated number of years of service before a person receives the full benefits of the plan. Private companies may offer other established plans as benefits.

The federal government has also established two plans in which you may participate. The 401(k) plan is a tax-deferred investment and savings plan. Many employers match what an employee invests. This allows you to defer, or delay, the taxes on your earnings until you retire. You pay taxes on the income and the gains the money has accrued when you withdraw the money from the plan, which can be done without penalty after the age of 59$\frac{1}{2}$.

The 403(b) is also a tax-deferred plan offered by nonprofit organizations such as public schools and city governments, who are unable to participate in the 401(k) plan. Employers generally do not match the funds of the employees in the 403(b) plan. The rules of the plan generally follow those of the 401(k).

Another tax-deferred investment is the IRA. Many different structures are available for this type of investment/retirement plan. Generally, an individual can invest up to $2,000 per year. Again, the taxes are deferred until you withdraw the money from the plan. Taxes are paid on the principal investment and its earnings over the years.

A recent type of IRA now available is the Roth IRA. A major difference between the Roth IRA and the regular IRA is that when you invest in the Roth IRA, you pay the taxes on the money when it is earned. When you withdraw the principal and its earnings at a later date, you do not pay taxes on either the principal or its earnings.

It is best to get advice from a reputable financial advisor when choosing your personal retirement plans.

Other Benefits. It seems as though there are as many categories of benefits as there are companies today. In addition to the benefits already mentioned, some companies offer health and fitness plans, day care, a variety of leave programs, stock options, annuity plans, free parking, job sharing, telecommuting, and so on. Many companies offer a wide variety of plans and permit the employee to choose the ones that best fit his or her needs. This is often referred to as a "cafeteria" of benefits.

Researching Salary/Wage Ranges

The vast majority of people choose to work to earn money that provides them with a living standard that is compatible with their value system. Therefore, salaries or wages earned by performing a particular job is certainly one of the critical factors that helps a person decide whether to accept a position. When you are researching careers and the path you want to take, you should certainly consider income. Rather than think in specific amounts, think in terms of ranges(for example, from $35,000—40,000 per year) because so many factors can affect the final offer. Certainly the region of the country or the country itself is a factor in what wages a company pays. The amount of experience you bring to a position and/or the level of education you have may also affect the salary you are paid.

The company itself has an influence on the amount a position is paid. For example, the average salary for an executive administrative assistant may average $32,000 to $38,000 per year. However, the annual salaries of administrative assistants in the successful high-tech industries may be much more than this. CEOs are also good examples. The president and CEO of a college or university may earn $80,000 to $150,000 a year. The president and CEO of a large American corporation may earn millions of dollars per year.

You have the responsibility to research and determine what a reasonable salary is for your chosen career field, in the region of the country in which you are searching, for the type and size of company you are considering, and for the level of education and experience you are bringing to the job.

A typical interview question is "What type of salary are you expecting?" Be prepared to answer this question. Provide a range, and be prepared to explain why you believe this amount to be reasonable. If you provide an amount that is too high, the employer will mentally put your résumé and application in "File 13" and erase your name from the shortlist of finalists for the position. If you provide an amount that is below the current acceptable level for that position and you are qualified for the job, the employer will agree to your amount. If you are willing to work for less than the norm, a company will happily pay you that amount. You may shortchange yourself of several thousand dollars a year, however.

Often you will see the salary question on a job application form. In this case, you have two choices. It is perfectly acceptable to write the word *negotiable* in the space provided. You may also provide the range that you discovered from your research. You may use either an annual salary or an hourly wage. Just be clear in the amount you are stating.

Evaluating Opportunity Costs

A person usually does not get everything he or she wants in a job offer. An opportunity cost is associated with the decision. Opportunity cost is an economic term that means you lose something in order to gain something else. For example, when you decide to purchase a new car using the money you have saved, the decision costs you the opportunity to gain interest on that money. So you must decide whether the opportunity cost is worth the purchase. Perhaps you purchase the new car so you have reliable transportation to a well-paying job.

When you are evaluating job offers, you must look at the opportunity costs, what you gain and what you lose by choosing to accept or reject the job offer. Of course, you want the scales to tip in favor of what you gain and minimize what you lose.

Thanking Your References

Send a letter to each of your references whether they have been contacted or not. Express your appreciation for their willingness to be a reference for you. Tell them about your new position and when you begin work. Give them a brief description of your job duties and responsibilities. Be sure to let them know how enthusiastic you are about the opportunities you foresee in this new adventure. Thank them again for their assistance. Your references will be grateful for the time you took to inform them of your job search results; they will be pleased they could be of help.

Expressing appreciation in writing to others for their assistance in helping you attain something you have worked toward is a part of professionalism. It is a good habit to form.

RECAP OF KEY CONCEPTS

- ◆ Corporate culture is the accumulation of unwritten rules of behavior, values, rules of engagement/procedures, and so on, that influence the way business is conducted in the workplace.
- ◆ You can get a sense of a company's corporate culture by determining the turnover rate and the type of reward system used by supervisors and by learning what a supervisor really wants.
- ◆ Benefits are offerings by a company that have value for the employee. Benefits provided by companies may include the following: Vacation/leave, bonuses, educational/professional development, health-care insurance, life-insurance, and retirement/pension plans.
- ◆ When researching salary and wage offers, be guided by the geographical area, your experience/education, the benefits offered, and the type and size of company.
- ◆ Opportunity cost is what is lost at the expense of what is gained. Consider what you gain versus what you lose by accepting a job offer.

6
Preparation for Change

 hange is inevitable and necessary. Where would you be without change in your life? Change means growth and hopefully improvement. Change may come in the form of a promotion or a different job in a different location. The word *change* is nearly synonymous with *stress* in the vocabulary of the new millennium. Negative connotations have become associated with change and stress, when in actuality change and stress can be positive motivators. Therefore, you must prepare yourself for change and develop an insurance policy to protect yourself and your career from any negative effects of change.

Upward Mobility

Upward mobility is the vertical movement from one level to the next in a career field. Upward mobility is accomplished by being promoted to the next level or by moving from one company to another with increased responsibility and authority. You move from job to job as you progress upward in your career.

Accepting an offer of a position with a company creates a mixture of emotions—excitement at the challenge of the new adventure, anticipation as you face the first day, anxiety about all you will be absorbing and learning, and fear of the unknown (even if you are accepting a new position in the company where you already work). These are all common emotions and very normal reactions to change.

Because your goal is to move upward in your career, you should begin to plan for promotions that will move you forward to greater responsibility and challenges. How do you know when the time is right for a job change? Certain signs and hints will give you an indication that it is time to change. What are the appropriate methods of initiating and implementing the job change? Make a job change while you are still working. Consult with selected members of your network about the impending job change. Leave behind strong and supportive bridges.

Change in the Workplace

Can you envision what you would be like if you never changed? What the world would be like if businesses didn't change? Many businesses no longer exist because they did not change. Royal and Underwood typewriters do not exist today because companies refused to recognize that electricity was coming to the typewriter industry. At one time, Britain's Triumph motor company was the world's leading manufacturer of motorcycles. But the company continued to use inefficient, old-fashioned production methods and outdated marketing and put little research into product development, while the Japanese modernized the motorcycle and produced it cheaper and to a higher standard.[8] Without a willingness to change, you may be left behind.

Therefore, change is a part of the workplace. What is important is learning how to deal with the change! Some changes are imposed upon you. Some changes you may initiate yourself. However the change comes, take advantage of the opportunity. The problem with change is that it often involves risk, and risk is threatening. When change involves risk, you experience either success or failure. In dealing with risk, you must learn how to handle the success or failure!

Insurance Policies for Change

The impact of change can be either positive or negative. Because change is such a pervasive factor in today's workplace, a wise employee begins to build strategies, or "insurance policies," against the negative effects of change. You can build in protection, or insurance, against change's negative effects in the following ways.

Being Perceived As a Valuable Employee. Establishing yourself as a valuable employee is equal to a job security insurance policy. Build a niche for yourself that would be difficult for the company to fill if you were to leave. Complete your work with excellence as your goal. Be an effective team player. In other words, determine what the company values in its employees, and become that employee.

Building Your Value. Accepting and starting work in a new position involves change. A new job may seem overwhelming during the first few weeks. How do you deal with the change and the new responsibilities? The best method of handling change is to develop effective work strategies. Four ways that can be effective are as follows:

1. **Use all of your senses to gather information.** Observation is vital in the first weeks at work. Carry a notebook with you, and make notes as you learn what tasks you are expected to perform. Nobody expects you to remember everything you are told. Listen to what is being said as well as what is not being said. Use your eyes to observe the body language of others and your ears to observe how people communicate with each other. Observe how people are dressed to learn about the dress code. Observe how employees and supervisors express courtesies and show respect. Observe how people interact. You can learn about the corporate culture and people's expectations just through observation. You can learn what is acceptable behavior within that environment.

2. **Ask.** Ask questions. Many organizations require that new employees attend an orientation program where policies and procedures of the company are explained. This is an opportunity to gain information that will help you adjust to the new workplace environment. Some information may need clarification. Do not hesitate to ask questions, and read any materials that are given to you. Avoid being critical. No one likes to hear from a new employee "This is the way we did it where I worked before." "When I was at Company A, we did…." Leave those remarks at home.

3. **Analyze.** As you feel more comfortable in your new arena, you should begin to analyze what you have learned and observed.

Then you may cautiously begin to ask why something is done a particular way. If the response is a logical explanation, the process or procedure may be acceptable. But if the response is "because this is the way we have always done it," the process or procedure may need to be revised.

4. **Read.** At the new employee orientation, basic policies and procedures will be explained to you—core hours for work, breaks and lunch, dress code, payroll, and leave and vacation. Not all policies will be covered, however. Do your homework. Get a copy of the policies and read them. Arm yourself against making an error that could be embarrassing to both you and your supervisor. If you discover a policy that is not clear, ask your supervisor for clarification. Doing so demonstrates that you have the initiative to learn on your own.

Displaying Initiative and Acclimating Yourself Quickly.

This strategy increases your value as an employee. The most expensive time for the employer is the time it takes the new employee to be trained for his or her position. So the quicker you learn to perform your job duties and to assume complete responsibility for them, the more valuable you become. Being a valuable employee is one of the best insurance policies against being negatively affected by change in a company.

Utilizing Effective Task Management Techniques.

No matter what your position in a company, you will be given tasks or projects to complete. The entire project may be your responsibility, or you may be accountable for only a portion of it. Regardless, your work must be completed accurately and in a timely manner. Someone is always waiting for your results. Become a person who is known for completing quality work on time.

Managing tasks you are assigned or you volunteer to do takes organization. It is not the task that you are managing, but yourself. Task management is self-management. Therefore, by organizing yourself, you are organizing the task.

- **Understand the purpose of the project or task.** By knowing the expectations of your supervisor regarding a project, you will be better focused on its completion within the guidelines that have been set.
- **Break the project down into manageable sections or tasks.**

- **Prioritize these smaller tasks.** Some tasks need to be done before others can be completed.
- **Create a time frame for the entire project or for each task.** Know when the project is due. Are you setting the due date, or has the due date already been established? Assign a time for the completion of each task on the prioritized list. Allow adequate time to complete each task.
- **If possible, set your own personal deadline or due date before the scheduled one.** This gives you time to review and revise the project to make sure it meets your standards of excellence.
- **Gather all the information you need to complete the task.**
- **Begin the first section or task.**
- **Keep to the time frame as closely as possible, but be flexible.** Some parts of the project may take longer than anticipated; some tasks may not take as much time.
- **Adjust the time frame as necessary.** However, always keep the deadline or due date in mind.

By establishing a reputation for completing quality projects in a timely manner, you increase your value as an employee. This is just another clause in the insurance policy for change.

Growing Professionally and Personally.

Another clause in this insurance policy for change is to establish job knowledge. A knowledgeable employee is a valuable employee. Therefore, take advantage of every opportunity to grow both personally and professionally.

Courtesy of ©PhotoDisc

- Be the first person to volunteer to learn a new software.
- Attend seminars and workshops to keep up with new trends in the business world, such as e-commerce.
- Join a professional organization and become active; take on a leadership role.
- Read professional magazines to learn what is happening in your marketplace.
- Know who your competitors are and what they are doing.

Becoming a Lifelong Learner.
Open the textbooks and go back to school (either paying for it yourself or taking advantage of assistance from your employer). You do not stop learning at a certain

point in time. In many cases, a degree from a college or university is only as good as the day it was issued. Technology is changing so rapidly and information is so readily available that learning can quickly become obsolete. For example, as an administrative assistant in the world of work today you must keep up with the changes in word processing software. Otherwise, you have poor marketable skills and would have difficulty finding a job. Everyone must keep learning. Yesterday's knowledge is useless; few people are marketable with old knowledge.

Dealing Effectively with Success and Failure. Success and failure are not mutually exclusive. You will experience both many times in your life. The important factor is to have more success than failure and to learn from both. Ben Sweetland said, "Success is a journey, not a destination."[9] Failure, however, is neither a destination nor a journey; it is only a speed bump in the road to success. Successful people look at failure as an opportunity and analyze the failure to see how they could have done it better.

The story goes that Thomas Edison made several thousand attempts at creating the lightbulb. When someone asked him how he felt about the thousands of failures, he replied that they weren't failures, but successful discoveries of several thousand ways *not* to invent the lightbulb.

Failure can be an attitude. How you deal with failure affects your value as an employee. If you persevere, learn what caused the failure, and eliminate the cause, you have turned a failure into a success. Dealing with success is equally as challenging. Many people gain success only to lose it because

Courtesy of ©PhotoDisc

they do not know how to control the effects of success. As with failure, analyzing why it happened puts the success into perspective. Remember that success is a journey, not a destination. Each success builds on the previous one and is the cornerstone of the next success.

By developing a strong insurance policy against the negative forces of change, you are protecting yourself from any negative impact on your personal and professional life. In addition, each of these strategies builds your self-confidence and the confidence your employer has in you, an essential foundation as you set yourself on the path for promotion.

Planning for a Promotion

In career planning, you are never static. You are continually preparing for the next step as you move up the career ladder. Looking ahead is important. The time will come when you want to instigate a change in your position and communicate your desire to move upward. Planning for promotion should begin the day you start your job. That does not mean you are so focused on the promotion or the next job that you do not perform well in your current job. Just the opposite: You perform so well in your current job that you are well prepared to move to the next job. In order to be prepared, consider the following ideas.

- **Find out what is important to your supervisor.** By listening carefully and observing, you should be able to determine the issues most important to your supervisor. Concentrate on those issues. Develop the skills and behaviors that are appreciated by your supervisor.

- **Keep records of your performance.** Over the lifetime of a job, your supervisor may not remember or may not know of all your successes. Over the lifetime of a job, you may not remember everything you accomplished. Save your calendars and to-do lists. At the end of each month, note the accomplishments you achieved during that period. Then at the end of the year (or better yet, when your performance appraisal is due) compile a complete list. Share this list with your supervisor before you meet for your performance review.

- **Offer to help.** Whether volunteering for a small task or a major project, your offer to help demonstrates initiative, and supervisors like initiative. Your offer also shows that you are more concerned about what is best for the company than what you want. This behavior is a subtle way of communicating to your supervisor that you are a team player and a company person who is willing to go the extra mile. You have not been so obvious as to ask for a promotion, but you are sending all the right signals that you are prepared to move ahead.

- **Request help from a mentor.** The importance of a mentor was discussed previously. Now is the time to request assistance from your mentor. He or she can help you along your career path by providing guidance and advice when you are in a dilemma about which path to choose. Your mentor will give you assistance in choosing the career path best suited to your ultimate goals.

- **Continue learning.** As was stated previously, be willing to learn, learn, and learn some more—on the job, in the classroom, at seminars and workshops, wherever and whenever the opportunity presents itself. By displaying your interest and enthusiasm for learning, you relay the subtle message to your supervisor that you want to learn and grow. You are sending a very positive message.

When employers look to promote someone to fill a position, they want a person who displays initiative, knows what is important, has a successful track record, and is willing to go the extra mile. By demonstrating these skills and behaviors, you may find yourself on the shortlist for a promotion.

When to Make the Job Change

You will have a sense of when it is time to leave a job. You will find yourself with a gut feeling or instinct that says, "Now is the time." You may have reached an impasse in some way; perhaps you are bored or frustrated or dissatisfied. Perhaps personal and professional growth have been stymied. Perhaps you feel the need to move into a new arena where new challenges and opportunities will be presented. Some of the reasons for leaving a job are explained below.

- **You reach the ceiling.** You have progressed as far as you can with the company. You have peaked. You have nowhere else to go. Any advancement within the company would depend on someone above you retiring, relocating, or being fired. You do not want to place your future in the hands of someone else, particularly when the situation begins with the word *if*. "If John retires" or "if Maria is promoted" are not the words upon which you want to rest your career.

Courtesy of ©PhotoDisc

- **You know of upcoming radical change.** If you know a major merger is coming, if the company has been discussing downsizing, or if the company's profit margin has not been meeting expectations, the time may be right to move on. Begin your job search before the event occurs. Plan and be prepared.
- **You are presented with an opportunity.** Even though you are employed, you still want to keep your network active and healthy.

Opportunity will knock if you have good ears and listen carefully. Evaluate another offer or possibility carefully in the context of where you currently are and where you can go. Do not ignore the knock.

- **You experience burnout.** When life seems out of control and the stress of work causes you to feel unmotivated or uninterested in what you are doing, you may be experiencing burnout. If this is the case, you need to seek help in coping with the problem. But burnout may also be an indication that you need to make a change.

How to Make the Job Change

Now that you have decided to make a change, you must begin the job search.

- **Search while you are working.** Once you have decided to make a job change, search for a new position while you are still working. Do not quit your job and then begin to look. It is easier to find a job while you have a job.

- **Leave behind strong, supportive bridges.** Do not leave a company in anger or frustration. Even though you may be experiencing strong negative emotions, do not let your employer know how you feel. You never know when you will need or want the assistance of a former employer. Be a professional, and maintain a good working relationship. Leave on good terms, and never bad-mouth the employer or the company you have left.

- **Write an effective letter of resignation.** The letter is notification of your resignation and should be addressed to the appropriate company employee. This procedure may be dictated by company policy.

  - The date of the letter should be the date of the notification of your resignation. If company policy dictates that the letter is not addressed to your immediate supervisor, be absolutely certain that he or she receives a copy of the letter too.

  - The first paragraph of the letter should state the fact that you are resigning from your position and the date your resignation will be effective. Company policy may require a notice of two-weeks or more. To maintain a positive relationship with the company, follow this policy. You may also want to give the company as much notice as possible and offer to be available for training your replacement. Also include a reason for leaving. You statement can be as brief as, "I have accepted a position with XYZ Company."

- In the final paragraph, state something positive about the company and your time with the company.
- Print the letter on letterhead stationery, and present it to the appropriate person in the organization.

Using these guidelines, you have followed company policy, have told why you are leaving, and have given positive feedback about the company. This will help you in establishing that all-important bridge with the former employer. You can leave your employer feeling confident that your past experiences will serve you well as you forge ahead in tackling your new position.

Rarely is the process of leaving one job to move to another a once-in-a-lifetime experience. You will face this process over and over again. Each experience provides you with the opportunity to gain more knowledge, face new challenges, and move comfortably along your career path.

RECAP OF KEY CONCEPTS

- Upward mobility is the vertical movement from one level to the next in a career field. Upward mobility is accomplished by being promoted to the next level or by moving from one company to another with increased responsibility and authority.
- Change must occur for progress to happen. Many companies no longer exist because they did not change.
- Establish an insurance policy to protect yourself against the negative effects of change. Be perceived as a valuable employee. Build your value by developing effective work strategies. Display initiative and acclimate yourself quickly to your job responsibilities. Learn to manage small tasks and major projects effectively. Become actively involved in your professional and personal growth. Become a lifelong learner. Learn to deal effectively with both success and failure.
- In preparing and planning for a promotion, know what is important to your supervisor, keep accurate and detailed

records of your accomplishments, volunteer to help, request help from a mentor, and continue learning.

◆ The time to make a job change is when you have reached the ceiling in a company and there is no room for you to grow further, when you know of upcoming radical change, or when you are presented with the right opportunity. If you should experience burnout, get help to cope with the situation, and realize it may be an indication that you need to make a change.

◆ When you know it is time to make a change, search for a new position while you are still working, maintain positive relationships with your current employer and supervisor, and write an effective letter of resignation at the appropriate time.

Endnotes

1. *Kiplinger Washington Letter,* 73, No.52, The Kiplinger Washington Editors, Washington, D.C., Dec. 1996.

2. Charles J.Givens, *Wealth Without Risk,* New York: Simon and Shuster, 1988. p. 21.

3. Joe Griffith, *Speaker's Library of Business Stories, Anecdotes, and Humor,* Prentice-Hall, Englewood Cliffs, New Jersey, 1990, p. 48.

4. http://career.ucsb.edu/

5. www.cisco.com/

6. Mark Golin, et.al; *Secrets of Executive Success: How Anyone Can Handle the Human Side of Work and Grow their Careers;* Rodale Press, Emmaus, Pennsylvania, 1991. p. 116.

7. *Webster's New World Dictionary, 2nd College Edition,* William Collins and World Publishing Company, Inc. 1978.

8. Joe Griffith, *Speaker's Library of Business: Stories, Anecdotes, and Humor,* Prentice Hall, Englewood Cliffs, New Jersey, 1990, p. 45-47.

9. Joe Griffith, *Speaker's Library of Business: Stories, Anecdotes, and Humor,* Prentice Hall, Englewood Cliffs, New Jersey, 1990, p. 341.

Online Resources

Self-Assessment and Interest Inventory
http://www.keirsey.com/cgi-bin/keirsey/newkts.cgi This site provides a short form of the Myers-Briggs Temperament Inventory. The assessment ·is not as accurate or as complete, but it is free.

Personality Inventory
http://www.users.interport.net/~zang/personality.html This is a fun site that provides a set of graphics. You receive a personality description based on your choice of the one that most appeals to you.

Guide to Résumé Writing
http://www.jobweb.org/catapult/guenov/res.html This site provides information about building an effective résumé. Sample résumés are also provided.

Job Interviewing
http://www.job-interview.net/ This comprehensive site provides interview questions and tips, dress guidelines, answers to interview questions, and so on.

Upward Mobility and Career Choices
http://family.med.und.nodak.edu/nata/placement/handbook/Upward.html This University of North Dakota site discusses career choices and provides a mini-assessment of interests and additional sites to visit for career planning assistance.

Note: These Web sites were operational at the time of printing. However, since the Web is continually changing, URLs can change or become inoperable. If you are unable to access these sites, use the following keywords to conduct your own Internet search:

Career planning

Upward mobility

Résumés

Corporate culture

Job interview

Portfolio Project

Purpose: To provide a comprehensive project that includes activities for each key concept presented in the *Career Planning and Networking module*. This project may be used by the participant as a resource tool for real-life career planning. The facilitator/instructor may also use this project as a part of the final assessment for this module.

Overview: The user will develop a portfolio by completing the designated activities below for each key concept presented in the module. The Portfolio should contain the following:

A Table of Contents for Your Portfolio

1. Topic 1
   a. Develop a list of individuals who could be members of your network.

2. Topic 2
   a. Include the results of a personal assessment taken at one of the Internet Web Sites
   b. Include a personal mission statement
   c. Include a total of four goals written as an activity in Topic 2— educational, financial, personal and career.

3. Topic 3
   a. Research a career of your choice. Write a short report outlining job availability, job titles, advancement possibilities, local salary/wage ranges, and required education.
   b. Research three companies in your local area (you may expand this to the career field). Provide as much information as you can about the company.
   c. Continue to add names (from companies) to the list of individuals in your current network developed in Topic 1. Define in what categories they might belong.

4. Topic 4

a. Develop a résumé.

b. Write a letter of application to accompany your résumé.

c. Develop a list of references.

d. Research and compile a list of ten interview questions.

e. Write a thank-you or follow-up letter.

5. Topic 5

a. Research three employer-offered benefits in which you would be interested. In a short report on each, provide a basic description of each. Then list the advantages and/or disadvantages of each.

b. Write a thank-you letter to one of your references.

6. Topic 6

a. Write a letter of resignation.

Post-Assesment Activity

Multiple Choice: Read each of the following statements carefully. Circle the letter of the best response for the following statements.

1. The standards or principles we use to help us make decisions or choices in our lives are
   a. societies.
   b. peers.
   c. value systems.
   d. missions.

2. A statement that describes what a company is, what it does, and how it envisions itself in relation to its market is a
   a. value system.
   b. mission.
   c. goal.
   d. market alignment.

3. When faced with making a decision and based on the importance of the factors involved in that decision, a good strategy is to
   a. verbalize.
   b. prioritize.
   c. personalize.
   d. quantify.

4. An excellent source of information about careers can be learned from
   a. college/career counselors.
   b. the Internet.
   c. government publications.
   d. all of the above.

5. The people who are connected to you through your career field
   a. are your career network.
   b. are a group.
   c. include only your friends and relatives.
   d. include only friends of friends and relatives of friends.

6. The person who is a teacher, coach, and helper, and who will help you learn about your career and career choices is a
   a. friend.
   b. mentor.
   c. relative.
   d. supervisor.

7. When planning a career, one should research
   a. vacation time.
   b. work relationships.
   c. job availability.
   d. all of the above.

8. A résumé should contain
   a. an objective.
   b. education/work experience.
   c. your name.
   d. all of the above.

9. A résumé that is organized in groups by types of experiences is a
   a. chronological résumé.
   b. curriculum vitae.
   c. functional résumé.
   d. none of the above.

10. An interview in which the interviewer(s) ask exactly the same questions in the same order to all the applicants is a(n)
   a. structured interview.
   b. unstructured interview.
   c. one-on-one interview.
   d. panel interview.

11. Appropriate attire for an interview includes clothing that is
   a. comfortable.
   b. conservative.
   c. clean.
   d. all of the above.

12. The purpose of the thank-you or follow-up letter is to
   a. tell the employer you are not interested in the position.
   b. ask for interview.
   c. keep your name and qualifications fresh in the employer's mind.
   d. all of the above.

13. The atmosphere, or environment, in which the work of the organization is completed is the
   a. corporate culture.
   b. grapevine.
   c. communication system.
   d. organizational structure.

14. Upward communication is the pathway in the company communication system in which
   a. the supervisor communicates with the subordinate.
   b. the subordinate communicates with the supervisor.
   c. the peer communicates with the peer.
   d. all of the above.

15. Offerings by a company that have value for the employee are
   a. communications.
   b. values.
   c. competition.
   d. benefits.

16. A tax-deferred investment and savings plan for retirement that permits the employer to match what the employee invests.
    a. IRA
    b. 401(k)
    c. 403(b)
    d. Roth IRA

17. The economic term that describes the loss of something in order to gain something else.
    a. gain/lose
    b. supply and demand
    c. negotiation
    d. opportunity cost

18. When beginning a new job, a helpful strategy for a successful beginning is to
    a. use your senses to learn as much as quickly as possible.
    b. ask questions and analyze processes.
    c. read company manuals to familiarize yourself with the policies.
    d. all of the above.

True-False: Read each of the following statements carefully. Circle T if the answer is true and F if the answer is false.

T F 1. A goal you are pursuing should be quantitative so you know if and when you have reached the goal.

T F 2. If there is a shortage of qualified workers in a career field, salary ranges will not differ.

T F 3. Newspapers provide very little information about companies and organizations, so you should avoid using them as a source.

T F 4. If a company is in litigation, the company's reputation, earning power, ability to hire and stability may be affected.

T F 5. Use a font size that is less than 10 for your résumé.

T F 6. When writing a solicited letter of application to a company or business, you do not know if a position is open.

T F 7. A letter of application should be one page and three paragraphs long.

T F 8. An interview is a meeting, usually face-to-face, between the employer and the job applicant.

T F 9. All interviews are one-on-one and face-to-face.

T F 10. The company grapevine is a rumor factory that is rarely accurate.

T F 11. Never use the word *negotiable* to answer the salary question on a job application form.

T F 12. The vertical movement from one level in a career field to the next is referred to as upward mobility.

Notes

Notes

Notes

Notes

Notes

Notes